D1479099

SPICY VEGAN

*A collection of delicious, spicy, original
Indian recipes*

Sudha Raina

ATHENA PRESS
LONDON

SPICY VEGAN
A collection of delicious, spicy, original Indian recipes
Copyright © Sudha Raina 2004

ISBN 1 84401 249 2

First Published 2004 by
ATHENA PRESS
Queen's House, 2 Holly Road
Twickenham, TW1 4EG
United Kingdom

Printed for Athena Press

SPICY VEGAN

A collection of delicious, spicy, original Indian recipes

I dedicate this book to my dear mother,
Mrs H K Haryana,
who inspired me at a young age
to cook all kinds of vegetarian food

Acknowledgements

My thanks are due to my dear husband and to my friend Kath who inspired me to write this book and helped me to complete my work. I am also grateful to my three lovely daughters and my son-in-law, all of whom persuaded me to write and complete this book.

Foreword

These spicy recipes for vegans and vegetarians do not contain any animal products. In this book, flexibility with measures and creativity with ingredients are of the greatest importance.

Easy availability of vegetables, fruits, spices and other ingredients used is one of my main considerations. Friends, relatives and sceptics will all appreciate this fresh, tasty and healthy vegan food. This book, with new ideas for vegans and vegetarians, contains approximately 133 delicious spicy recipes, based mainly on north Indian home cooking.

I hope you will try these tasty recipes, and wish you many years of enjoyable spicy cooking

Contents

Introduction

I have always been a vegetarian, and I have been cooking since I was fourteen years old. My mum and grandma hated cruelty to animals. I wanted to write an easy cookery book for people who do not like using animal products. Some people are allergic to dairy products, and some do not want to use them for moral reasons. Vegans believe in compassion and gentleness towards all living beings. Essential minerals and vitamins can be found in many different foods, so it is not difficult to be a vegan.

I used to teach Hindi to one of my friends. At that time she was a vegetarian, but now she is a staunch vegan. I must confess that she is the one who inspired me to write this book.

India is a vast country with a huge population, most of which depends on agriculture for a living. There you will find all sorts of food; vegetarian, non-vegetarian and vegan. There are hundreds of varieties of vegetarian and vegan dishes.

Spicy Vegan contains delicious recipes for those who enjoy spicy and tasty food. This food is really easy to cook. People might think this mixture of various exotic spices is very complicated, but it isn't. I have tried to present these recipes in a simple manner, so that they are easy to understand and you will enjoy cooking them. There are no hard and fast rules. You will enjoy preparing a mixture of spices, vegetables and herbs. Once you become accustomed to this type of cooking, you are bound to become a slave to the exotic flavours for ever.

Balanced Diet

There are many soya bean products available in the shops today. However, some people are allergic to these. Also, some soya bean products are genetically modified. Therefore, I have attempted to cater to vegan tastes with spicy, palatable and delicious food, using a minimum amount of soya products.

To balance a vegan diet it is essential to eat some foods from the following groups each day or on a regular basis:

HERBS, VEGETABLES AND FRUITS – important for many vitamins and minerals.

CEREALS AND GRAINS – these are essential for energy, fibre, B vitamins, calcium and iron.

PULSES, NUTS AND SEEDS – important for protein, energy, fibre, calcium, iron and zinc. Some people may be allergic to nuts, so they must avoid them.

OILS AND MARGARINE – contain essential fatty acids, and vitamins A and E.

Vitamins

Each vitamin has a specific and important role in the body, and its deficiency can cause serious illness or weakness.

VITAMIN A – considered good for vision and skin. It is found in carrots, apricots, melon and green leafy vegetables.

VITAMIN B GROUP – believed to provide immunity for the heart and nervous system. It is important for healthy skin and a good digestive system. Many people think that vegans lack vitamin B12; however, it can be found in yeast extract, fortified cereals and margarine.

VITAMIN C – considered necessary for strong gums and healthy skin. It increases immunity and helps the absorption of iron from food. Citrus fruits such as oranges, lemons and grapefruit provide a large amount of vitamin C. Strawberries, blackcurrants, tomatoes, peppers, potatoes and cauliflower are also a good source.

VITAMIN D – thought to play a vital part in the formation of teeth and bones. The main source is plenty of sunshine. It is also contained in fortified vegan margarine and cereals.

VITAMIN E – considered essential for cell formation and tissues. Vegetable oils, wheatgerm, nuts, seeds and margarine are good sources.

FOLIC ACID – thought to be very important, especially in pregnancy. It can be obtained from green leafy vegetables, whole grains, cereals, nuts (some people are allergic to nuts), beans, yeast extract and all kinds of fruit.

Minerals

Minerals such as calcium, magnesium, phosphorus, potassium, sodium, iron, sulphur and zinc are very important for good health. They boost the immune system and strengthen bones and teeth.

To keep these minerals in balance, you need to include in your diet on a regular basis foods such as sesame seeds, sunflower seeds, nuts, pulses, whole grain cereals, fresh and dried fruit, vegetables, cocoa, brown rice, bread and yeast extract.

Herbs

Herbs are known to have therapeutic qualities. Ancient Egyptians used many herbal medicines. *Ayurvedic* medicines have been famous in India since ancient times. Different herbs have different effects on food and drink. They are used for aroma, taste and decoration. Herbs are full of medicinal properties and flavour. In India some herbs are cooked as vegetables; for example fenugreek leaves and fennel leaves. Some of the popular Indian herbs are:

BASIL (*TULSI*) – very popular in Mediterranean countries such as Italy and also in India. It is commonly used in pizzas. Basil tea is good for colds and digestion.

BAY LEAF (*TEJ PATTA*) – used in masaala vegetables, daal, pickles and garam masaala.

CORIANDER (*DHANIYA*) – green leaves mostly used as decoration and flavour for masaala vegetables, salads and chutneys. Coriander can be eaten raw. It is considered good for the heart and for some infections, and can help prevent flatulence.

FENNEL (*SAUNF*) – fennel tea has a relaxing and calming effect. Its green leaves are used as *saag* on their own or along with *methi* (fenugreek) leaves. *Saag* is a general Indian term for any semi-liquid or dry, leafy vegetable dish.

MINT (*PODINA*) – these thick, dark-green leaves are used for making chutneys and for decoration, and are a good aid for digestion.

Vegetables (*sabzian*)

Green leafy vegetables are said to be one of the main sources of a beautiful and healthy body and mind. In Indian mythology, Rishis and Munis (learned sages of ancient India) lived very long lives eating only vegetables and fruits. However, doctors and nutritionists do not advise this, as protein is also needed in a healthy diet.

Salads are very low in calories. They contain a great deal of water yet provide many nutrients such as vitamins, calcium and iron.

As far as possible we should try to avoid tinned and ready-made food, because this type of food may contain preservatives, colourings and flavourings.

Vegetables supply our body with many vitamins, minerals and carbohydrates. They are an excellent source of vitamins A and C, low in cholesterol and high in fibre. They are mostly low in calories. Dark green vegetables especially are a good source of calcium. All vegetables have different qualities, so we should try to eat a large variety. It is believed that they lower the risk of heart disease, cancer, diabetes, blood circulation problems and hypertension, as well as protecting the eyesight. Vegetables are good eaten raw or cooked.

It is better to buy younger and smaller vegetables because the more tender the vegetable the sweeter the taste. Vegetables should be eaten as soon as possible after purchasing.

Potatoes are a good source of energy. They should be firm. Never buy soft potatoes or potatoes with any green tinge.

Clean all vegetables thoroughly before cooking. It is easier to clean leeks and spring onions if you slit them lengthwise and wash them two or three times.

To keep the maximum nutrients, it is essential to cook

vegetables in the minimum quantity of water. Do not overcook the vegetables.

In this book I have used the following vegetables (Indian equivalents in brackets):

AUBERGINE (*BAINGAN*) – a very versatile vegetable. It is full of iron and considered good for the liver and stomach. There are many varieties of aubergines, but the most popular ones are small or baby aubergines with shiny black or purple skin, and long or round aubergines with shiny reddish-blue, purple-blue or dark-blue skin.

BEAN SPROUTS (*LUNGI*) – contain iron and most of the vitamin B group.

BEETROOT (*CHUKANDAR*) – full of iron and sugar. It is good for salads.

OKRA (*BHINDI*) – a green vegetable with vitamin A.

BITTER GOURD (*KARELA*) – rich in iron. Thought to be good for people with diabetes.

BROCCOLI – an excellent source of vitamins A and C, iron and calcium.

CABBAGE (*BANDH GOBHI*) – it is said that cabbage has an ingredient which can help to reduce stomach ulcers. Cabbage is rich in iron and vitamin A. It is a good source of fibre and is low in calories.

CAPSICUMS, OR PEPPERS (*SHIMLA MIRCH*) – it is believed that capsicums contain three times as much vitamin C as lemons or oranges, and have strong antioxidant properties, which may prevent the development of cancer. You can eat them in various forms, as salads, chutney or as a cooked vegetable.

CARROTS (*GAAJAR*) – a good source of vitamin A, fibre, iron and natural sugar.

CAULIFLOWER (*PHOOL GOBHI*) – full of vitamin C. Brussels sprouts and broccoli are also from the same family. Cauliflower is a low-calorie vegetable. Spices make it tasty, nutritious and easily digestible.

CELERY – contains iron. It is good if eaten raw.

COURGETTES (*GHIA TOREE*) – have a high water content. They are easily digestible, low in calories and full of vitamins A and C.

CUCUMBER (*KHEERA*) – has a high water content. It is tasty when fresh and crisp.

FENNEL LEAVES (*SOA* or *SONF*) – rich in vitamin C and iron. Fennel leaves and small, dark-green fenugreek leaves are a good mixture for a lovely aroma and a pleasant taste. Fennel leaves are considered good for digestion.

FENUGREEK LEAVES (*METHI*) – small, dark-green leaves with a lovely fragrance. They are thought to be rich in iron.

GOURD (*LAUKI* or *GHIA*) – an easily digestible vegetable.

GREEN CHILLI (*HARI MIRCH*) – rich in vitamin C and considered effective against catarrh.

HORSERADISH (*MOOLI*) – fresh horseradish is good for the liver. If you keep grated horseradish for too long it develops a very strong smell, which some people may not like.

KOHLRABI (*GANTH GOBHI*) – a good source of vitamin C and fibre. It is said that it helps to reduce cancer. Kohlrabi belongs to the cabbage, cauliflower and broccoli family.

LEEKS (*BHUKEIN*) – a versatile vegetable containing iron.

LEMONS (*NIMBU*) – rich in vitamin C, which is very important for the immune system.

LETTUCE (*HARAA PATTA* or *SALAAD PATTA*) – good for salads because of the lightness of the leaf. It contains iron and has a high water content.

MARROW (*PHOOT*) – a light and easily digestible vegetable. It has a high water content.

MUSHROOMS (*KHUMBI*) – contain potassium. They have a good flavour.

ONIONS (*PIAZ*) – considered beneficial for lowering blood cholesterol. They are said to be a good decongestant.

PEAS (*MATTAR*) – thought to be the oldest vegetable. They have a high iron content.

POTATOES (*AALOO*) – a good source of potassium and vitamin C.

PUMPKIN (*SITAPHAL* or *KADDU*) – high in vitamin A. It can be used for sweet and savoury dishes.

RUNNER BEANS (*PHALIAN*) – a good source of iron, zinc, magnesium and vitamin E. Green beans are full of protein and fibre. French beans, runner beans, broad beans and dwarf beans can all be cooked in the same manner.

SMALL GOURD (*TINDA*) – a variety of gourd. It contains vitamins A and C. It is a low-calorie, easily digestible vegetable with a light-green to whitish colour. Gourds come in many shapes and sizes – long (*lauki* or *ghia*), round and very small. Small round ones are called *tindas*.

SPINACH (*PAALAK*) – a good source of vitamins A and C. It has been suggested that eating dark-green leafy vegetables gives protection against cancer.

SWEET POTATOES (*SHAKARKANDI*) – high in vitamin A and calcium. They can be used in sweet and savoury dishes.

TOMATOES (*TAMAATAR*) – a good source of vitamins C and E. They are believed to contain an ingredient which can prevent cancer. Actually, tomatoes are a fruit rather than a vegetable.

TURNIPS (*SHALGAM*) – a low-calorie vegetable with a high water content. Turnips are a useful source of vitamin C and fibre.

YAM (*JIMIKAND*) – a good source of potassium and protein. It is pale white in colour.

Fruit (*phal*)

Fresh fruit is a very important part of our daily food. Some fruits are sweet and some fruits are sour. They all contain different vitamins and minerals. Fruit is mostly low in calories and provides vitamin C, which is very important for our immune system. It is considered essential for healthy skin.

APPLE (*SEB*) – a low-calorie fruit. High in fibre, they are considered to be helpful in the treatment of constipation and diarrhoea. There are many varieties of apples (for example: Cox, Red Delicious, Bramley, Royal Gala, Golden Delicious, Granny Smith and Empire). Granny Smith and Bramley are good for cooking. Apples are excellent for making chutneys.

APRICOTS (*KHURMAANI*) – you can eat them fresh or dried. Both are good for the health. They are full of vitamin A, iron and fibre.

BANANAS (*KELE*) – a good source of fibre and potassium. It is believed that bananas are good for healing ulcers. They contain a high level of sugar.

BERRIES – these low-calorie fruits are full of vitamin C.

CHERRIES – there are many varieties of cherries – morello, sweet cherries and hybrid cherries. They are a good source of potassium and vitamin C.

FIG (*ANGEER*) – This calcium- and fibre-rich fruit can help prevent constipation.

GRAPES (*ANGOOR*) – a good source of potassium. Black grapes contain antioxidants, but they can sometimes induce migraine. Black grape juice is a good source of iron.

GUAVA (*AMROOD*) – an exotic tropical fruit, full of vitamin C, potassium and fibre. It is thought to be very good for the skin and has an excellent aroma.

JAAMUN – a dark-purple coloured, plum-shaped Indian fruit available in July and August, during the monsoon season in India.

KIWI FRUIT – full of vitamin C, and good for decoration.

LOQUATS (*LUKAAT*) – mixed taste of apple and apricot.

LYCHEES (*LEECHIES*) – this originally Chinese fruit is quite a good source of vitamin C and it makes a good dessert.

MANGO (*AAM*) – a very versatile fruit with vitamins A and C. Eat it when it is well ripened. Raw mangoes can be used in pickles and chutneys. Indian mangoes are known to have some of the finest flavours and tastes.

MELON (*KHARBOOZAA*) – contains a large amount of water, so it is good for the kidneys. Melon is a nutritious appetiser.

ORANGE (*MALTA*) – this excellent source of vitamin C is beneficial for the immune system and heart. Its fresh fragrance makes everybody cheerful.

PAPAYA (*PAPEETAA*) – full of medicinal value and easily digestible.

PEACH (*AAROO*) – this low-calorie, easily digestible fruit has high vitamin A and C content, and is very good for the skin.

PEARS (*NAASHPAATI* OR *NAAKH*) – rich in vitamin C, fibre, potassium, natural sugar and pectin. There are some soft and some hard varieties. *Bagugosha* is very soft and juicy. *Naashpaati* is a little hard but very sweet. It is good for digestion.

PHALSA – an Indian fruit like dark purple berries

PINEAPPLE (*ANANAAS*) – a very juicy, sweet and tasty fruit.

PLUM (*ALOOCHAA*) – dried plums are called prunes.

POMEGRANATE (*ANAAR*) – its seeds are full of vitamin C and fibre. It is considered a symbol of fertility.

STRAWBERRIES – have a high vitamin C content. In herbal folklore it is said that strawberries are a good remedy for kidney stones and have antibacterial properties.

WATERMELON (*TARBOOZ*) – contains a great deal of water. It has a very juicy and sweet taste. After eating watermelon avoid drinking water as it might give you a stomach pain.

Fresh fruits can be eaten at any time – breakfast, lunch, tea or as a snack.

Pulses (*daal*)

Pulses are beans, peas, and lentils, which are preserved by drying. They are a good source of fibre, protein and energy. Pulses are very nutritious and provide most of the proteins and fibre we need. Especially if you are not a meat eater, you should include them with your main meals. They should be stored in an airtight container. They are good if eaten in liquid (easier to digest). Add a dash of lemon to make them more appetising.

Pulses can be soaked overnight or cooked for a longer time. Kidney beans and soya beans need a long time to cook – at least 1 to 1½ hours. The quantity of dried beans and lentils approximately doubles during soaking and cooking. In supermarkets and convenience stores you can buy canned beans and lentils which are quicker to use.

Sprouted beans are rich in protein, fibre, minerals and vitamin C.

I have used the following pulses in my recipes:

BLACK-EYED BEANS (white beans with a black mark).

BLACK GRAM (*KAALE CHANE* – dark brown) – people think this is chickpea but it is not. It resembles chickpea in shape but has a totally different colour and taste and is a little smaller. It has a dark reddish-brown colour. *Chana daal* is made of gram, and *besan* (gram flour) is made of *chana daal*. Gram is full of protein and iron. You can buy it at an Indian grocer's. Soak a cup of black gram overnight and boil it in the morning until the gram becomes tender. Take out a cup of the liquid and add a little salt (according to taste), black pepper and a few drops of lemon, and drink it. It is a very good remedy for colds and it is delicious. The boiled black gram can also be eaten whole after the liquid has been drained, with a dash of lemon and salt. Sprouted black gram is very healthy if you eat it with a dash of lemon and salt. There are so many things you can make with whole black gram and gram flour. Gram flour is a little salty. If you eat *chapaatis* or *paraathas* (made of this flour) with vegan yoghurt without adding any salt or sugar it is very good for itchy skin. Black gram is very popular in India.

BLACK GRAM – SPLIT (*CHANA DAAL* – yellow without husk)

CHICKPEAS OR *SAFED CHANE* (off-white colour)

MASOOR – whole (dark-brown disc shape)

MASOOR LENTILS – split (*DAAL* – pinkish-orange)

MOONG BEANS – whole (round dark green)

MOONG BEANS – split (*DAAL* with green husk)

MOONG BEANS – split, washed or *DHULI MOONG DAAL* (light yellow without husk)

RED KIDNEY BEANS – (*RAJMA* – red-skinned beans)

SOYA BEANS (round, cream-coloured beans) – very versatile. They are healthy as long as not genetically modified, and they are full of vitamins and protein. You can buy many soya products in the shops these days. The most popular products are soya flour, soya milk, soya sauce and tofu. However, some people are allergic to these products.

URAD – whole (round black)

URAD – split (*DAAL* with black husk)

URAD – split, washed or *DHULI URAD* (*DAAL* – white without husk)

Nuts (*sukha mewa*)

Nuts are full of protein, carbohydrate and oils. However, some people are allergic to nuts. There are many types of nuts, including:

ALMONDS (*BADAAM*)
BRAZIL NUTS
CASHEW NUT (*KAAJU*)
COCONUT (*NAARIAL*)
PEANUTS (*MOONG PHALI*)
PINE NUTS (*CHILGOZE*)
PISTACHIO (*PISTA*)
WALNUT (*AKHROT*)

Nuts can be used as flakes or pieces, or ground. Roasting and frying enhances their flavour and they can be added to salads. Cashew nuts, pistachios, almonds, peanuts and pine nuts have a wonderful aroma after roasting, and can be eaten as snacks.

It is not necessary to use nuts in the main meal, because some people are allergic to them. It is better to serve them separately so that those allergic to them can avoid them.

Seeds (*beej*)

Seeds are good for their nutty taste and flavour. You can use them in salads, breads and sweets.

Always use a heavy, thick-based pan for frying or roasting seeds.

The following are popular varieties of seeds:

SESAME SEEDS (*TIL*)
POPPY SEEDS (*POST*)
SUNFLOWER SEEDS (*SURYAMUKHI BEEJ*)
PUMPKIN SEEDS (*KADOO BEEJ*)

You can use them in any type of cooking or salads.

Grains

There are many varieties of grains, which are used in different parts of the world:

- MAIZE (*MAKKI*) – this is said to be gluten-free. It is used for making corn meal flour, popcorn and Indian bread (*chapaatis* or *paraathas*).

- MILLET (*BAJRAA*) – this can be cooked just like rice or pilau. Its flour, which is said to be gluten-free, can be used for flat breads (sweet or savoury).

- OATS (*JUAAR*) – oats are considered to be very good for the skin because they contain oil and proteins. They are gluten-free so they are good for people who are allergic to gluten.

- RICE (*CHAAWAL*) – rice is eaten in many parts of the world – for example, in Sri Lanka, India, China, Burma, Thailand, Indonesia, Japan and Nepal. It is the staple diet in these countries and is a good source of protein and carbohydrate. In many eastern and Asian countries, people believe rice is auspicious, a sign of fertility and full of life and health. There are many varieties of rice, including basmati, easy-cook, long-grain, brown and pudding rice.

WHEAT (*GANDHAM* or *GEHUN*) – wheat is mostly used for bread, pancakes, biscuits and pasta. Coarse semolina, fine semolina and couscous are used to make food with different tastes in different regions. Wheat (medium) flour and wholemeal flour are very healthy because they contain bran and wheatgerm, making them rich in fibre and vitamins A and B. In my recipes I have mostly used wheat (medium) flour.

Oils (*tel*)

We should not eat too much oil, but a certain amount is necessary for our bodies. It supplies essential fatty acids and vitamins.

Oils are contained in nuts, seeds and pulses. There are many varieties of oils such as mixed vegetable, peanut, corn, safflower, sunflower, olive, rapeseed, sesame seed and soya bean. I mostly use corn oil or sunflower oil, but you can use any oil of your choice.

Spices (*masaale*)

Spices are very good for your digestion, with their wonderful aroma and taste. For hundreds of years, spices have also been used as a cure for several ailments. Their distinctive colour and flavour stimulate the palate and enhance the appetite.

AJWAIN – this seed has a lovely aroma. The seeds are smaller than cumin seeds.

ASAFOETIDA (*HING*) – this is the processed gum of a plant, used powdered for its aroma. Always use just a pinch. It has a very strong smell and some people may not like its raw odour. Keep it tightly covered while storing. You can buy it at most Indian grocers.

BAY LEAF (*TEJ PATTA*) – this leaf has a mellow flavour and is used dried as a spice in cooking.

BLACK PEPPER (*KAALI MIRCH*) – this mildly hot spice has a pungent taste and is used either whole or ground.

CARDAMOM (*ILAAICHI*) – this aromatic dry fruit, containing seeds, has two varieties, green and black. Green is mostly used in sweets, and black in savoury dishes.

CAYENNE PEPPER POWDER (*DEGI MIRCH*) – this has a very dark-red colour and a pungent but not very hot taste. It is good for giving rich red colour to dishes.

CHILLIES (*MIRCH*) – chillies are small hot peppers with a pungent taste. Generally, the smaller the pepper the hotter it is. They can be used whole, chopped, as a paste or in powdered form in many recipes, including *daal*, *masaala* vegetable dishes, chutneys and pickles.

CINNAMON (*DAAL CHEENI*) – this is the aromatic bark of a tree of the laurel family used as spice. You can make tea by infusing this bark. It is thought to be good for the throat.

CLOVE (*LAVANG*) – clove is a dried flower bud, which is used as a spice. It is said to have medicinal value. Its oil is a good remedy for gum pain. If you make tea by infusing one or two cloves in it, it is considered good for the treatment of colds and coughs.

CORIANDER SEEDS (*DHANIYA BEEJ*) – dried coriander seeds are used whole, crushed or powdered to add flavour to many dishes. They have a wonderful aroma.

CUMIN SEEDS (*ZEERA*) – these aromatic seeds are used for flavour. They also make food easier to digest.

FENNEL SEEDS (*SAUNF BEEJ*) – fennel seeds are used as a spice. These fragrant seeds are from a yellow flowered herb with fine leaves, and are used as flavouring.

FENUGREEK SEEDS (*METHI BEEJ*) – fenugreek is an aromatic plant. Its leaves and seeds are used in different types of cooking. The leaves can be used for savoury *paraathas* or vegetable dishes. The seeds are used as a spice for flavouring.

GARLIC (*LAHSUN*) – this has a pungent taste and is much used for flavouring in cookery. It is considered a protection against heart disease.

GINGER (*ADRAK*) – this has a hot taste and a mild flavour, and is much used as flavouring in cookery. It is said to be a good remedy for colds.

MANGO POWDER (*AMCHOOR*) – made by grinding dried, raw mangoes. It has a very sour taste and enhances aroma in certain dishes.

MUSTARD SEEDS (*SARSON*) – these are brownish-yellow in colour and have a lovely nutty aroma. They are used whole, crushed, roasted and fried to add flavour to *masaala* vegetable dishes. They are also used as a paste or spicy condiment.

SAFFRON (*KESAR*) – these small stigmas are used for a lovely aroma, colour and flavouring. Saffron is mostly used for desserts such as semolina halwa, sweet rice and rice pudding.

SESAME SEEDS (*TIL*) – black sesame seeds are the source of sesame oil. They are also used in savoury and sweet dishes. These seeds are rich in calcium and have a pleasant, nutty taste.

TAMARIND (*IMLI*) – this fruit, with an acid pulp, is used to make chutney, preserves or a cooling drink. It gives a tangy taste to *sambhar*.

TURMERIC POWDER (*HALDI*) – this is a ginger family plant native to India. It gives a beautiful yellow colour to food and is full of aroma.

MIXTURE OF SPICES

The following mixture of spices is used mainly to enhance the aroma in cooking or to decorate the dish when served.

GARAM MASAALA

Garam masaala consists of black pepper, black cardamom, bay leaf, cinnamon, cumin seeds and coriander powder. (You can obtain packs of this ground mixture at any Indian grocer's.) You can also buy it as pre-packed whole spices and grind them at home. It is used extensively in Indian cookery.

TASTY AND APPETISING MASAALA *(BUKNU)*

This masaala can be sprinkled over cooked food. It is very tasty and full of aroma.

½ tsp hing
6 tsp cumin seed powder
3 tsp coriander powder
2 tsp mango powder
1 tsp salt
¼ tsp black salt (you can buy this at an Indian grocer's)

Roast the *hing* for 1 minute, then add the cumin seed and coriander powder and roast for another minute (keep stirring). Grind them and mix in the salt, black salt (*kaala namak*), and mango powder. Keep it in a bottle. Use it whenever you want to sprinkle something spicy on your food or snack. You can even sprinkle it on your toast. Just use a pinch or two.

Tips for the Kitchen

- When cooking cabbage add a few grains of sugar. It will give a good taste and colour.

- Soak lentils for half an hour or longer before cooking to save fuel and time.

- You can add extra water when cooking lentils, kidney beans or chickpeas.

- Purée some fresh garlic (liquidise or shred) and store it in a bottle in the fridge for a week.

- Slice onions finely, fry them and store them in a bottle in the fridge for a week.

- These fried onions can be used for any vegetable or *daal* dish.

- Grind or grate ginger and store in a bottle in the fridge for a week.

- When you are in a hurry you can use it for cooking liquid *masaala* dishes.

- You can knead some dough and cover it with cling film or with a tight lid and keep in the fridge for 2–3 days. When you want to use it, just take it out 10–15 minutes beforehand.

- When you are kneading flour for plain *chapaatis* or *paraathas,* you can add one or two spoonfuls of sesame seeds for nourishment, if you wish.

Cooking Methods

There are many methods of cooking. Different types of food need different types of cooking. Some methods of cooking Indian food are:

BOILING – this method can be used for rice, pasta, pulses and vegetables.

STEAMING – vegetables or fruits can be cooked by putting them in a steamer over boiling water.

FRYING ON A *TAVA* OR GRIDDLE – is very common in Indian cookery. Different types of bread (e.g. *chapaatis, paraathas*), pancakes and snacks are made in this way (with a few drops of oil or vegetable ghee applied on either side).

SHALLOW FRYING – means frying with a little oil. Shallow frying is useful for cutlets and snacks.

DEEP FRYING – frying with a large amount of oil in a wok or *karahi*. This method is useful for chips, *pooris* (Indian fried bread,) *samosas* and *pakoras*. (Ensure that you do not overheat the oil and always take care to protect yourself from the risk of burning.)

ROASTING – there are two methods of roasting: oven (potatoes, sweet potatoes, aubergine, vegetable tikka, kebabs), and over a flame or on a *tava* or griddle, known as dry roasting (spices, semolina, coffee beans or any type of nuts or vegetables).

GRILLING – cooking under a grill (bread snacks, grilled vegetables, grilled toast with vegetables on top).

USING MASAALA SAUCE – this is a liquidised mixture of various spices, garlic, ginger and green chilli. Add a little water to the ingredients (according to the recipe) in the liquidiser. After frying this paste, add other spices and water. This sauce is mostly used for liquid or semi-liquid dishes.

LIQUID AND DRY DISHES – liquid and semi-liquid dishes are made with masaala sauce. Dry dishes can be made using water, but after cooking most of the liquid should have evaporated.

Important Notes

In my recipes I have used vegetables, spices and other ingredients which are tried, safe and delicious, based on my lifelong experience. If, however, you are allergic to any of the ingredients or do not like them, avoid using them.

Special care must be taken while cooking – particularly while frying – so that there is no risk to the person.

Ventilate the kitchen well while cooking, otherwise the aroma could spread to other rooms.

A special feature of Indian food is that it is mostly cooked on open heat, not in the oven. There are some varieties of bread, such as *naan* and *tandoori roti*, which are cooked in a clay-lined open oven called a *tandoor*. At home when you do not have a *tandoor* you can cook them using a *tava* (griddle).

You should ensure that you have the following items available in your kitchen for Indian cookery. The quantity you buy and keep will depend on your own requirements:

- Fresh fruits
- Dry fruits
- Vegetables
- Onions
- Potatoes
- Garlic
- Cooking oil
- Ajwain (its seeds are smaller than cumin seeds)
- Cinnamon (*daal cheeni*)
- Coriander seeds (*dhaniya* – whole and powdered)

- Cumin seeds (*zeera*)
- Dried fenugreek leaves (*kasuri methi*) available in small packs at Indian grocer's
- Dried red chilli (*laal mirch* – both whole and powdered)
- Fennel seeds (*saunf*)
- Fenugreek seeds (*methi*)
- Garam masaala (mixture of cumin, cloves, cardamom, black pepper and coriander)
- Asafoetida (*hing*) – available as *hing* powder at Indian grocers. This spice is optional in all my recipes as some people may not like its odour
- Black pepper (*kaali mirch* – whole and powdered)
- Tamarind pulp or fruit (*imli*)
- Tomato purée
- Turmeric powder (*haldi*)
- Salt (*namak*)
- Sugar (*cheeni*)
- Corn meal flour (*makki ka atta*)
- Gram flour (*besan*)
- Semolina (*suji*)
- Wheat flour (medium *chapaati* flour)
- Plain white flour (*maida*)
- Pulses of your choice (*daal*)
- Rice (*chaawal*)
- Griddle (*tava* – for cooking)
- Wok (*karahi* – for deep-frying)
- Tongs (*chimta* – to hold *chapaatis* and *paapad* while cooking)
- Grinder (for spices)
- Liquidiser (for making liquid masaala)

(Note: if you cannot obtain any of these items at your local store you can buy them at an Indian grocer's.)

In these recipes *avoid* using:

- *Hing* and garlic together, as they would give a very strong flavour
- More than one or two green chillies, unless you want very hot food
- A tightly closed lid when cooking lentils with a large quantity of liquid (it will boil over and make a mess)

When cooking rice, *do not* stir again and again, as it will break the grains.

In most of my recipes I have used approximate amounts of ingredients, but you can alter them according to your requirements after you have had some experience. Cooking is an adventure. Once you learn the basis of a recipe, you can make alterations easily. With a mixture of herbs, vegetables, pulses, oils, grains and spices you can make delicious food for your family, friends and guests.

Equivalent Measures (approximate)

Dry Weight

1 oz	=	28 g
8 oz	=	225 g
16 oz	=	453 g

Liquid Weight

1 fl oz	=	28 ml
5 fl oz / ¼ pint	=	140 ml
10 fl oz / ½ pint	=	284 ml
20 fl oz /1 pint	=	568 ml

In my recipes, for measures I have used teaspoon, tablespoon and cup (average teacup, not mug). All these measures are approximate.

1 teaspoon	=	5 ml
1 tablespoon	=	15 ml
1 cup	=	200 g

The quantities in all my recipes are for four people. However, you can change these quantities a little if you wish.

Abbreviations

g – gram(s)
kg – kilogram(s)
ml – millilitre(s)
tsp – teaspoon(s)
tbs – tablespoon(s)

Starters and Snacks

SAMOSAS

NAMAKPAARE

Starters and Snacks

Starters and Snacks

For starters, you can use the following ready-made savoury dishes if you do not want to cook:

BOMBAY MIX

ROASTED PISTACHIOS

SALTED CASHEW NUTS

FRIED SPICED *DAAL* (*moong* or *gram daal*) available at Indian stores

FRIED OR ROASTED PEANUTS

FRIED *PAAPAD* (called pappadoms in south India)

BHELPOORI

Ingredients

250 g sev (made of gram flour, shaped like small vermicelli – available prepared at most Indian grocers')
250 g puffed rice
5–6 medium potatoes (boiled, peeled and cut into very small pieces)
2 cucumbers (washed and cut into small pieces)
2–3 onions (chopped into small pieces)
2–3 lemons (halved – use according to taste)
½ tsp black salt (optional)
salt (according to taste)
2 tsp red chilli powder (according to taste)
½ tsp hing (roasted)
4–5 tsp cumin seeds (roasted and ground)
sweet and sour tamarind and prune chutney

METHOD

Mix together the potatoes, cucumbers, onions, chopped coriander and salt in a large bowl.

Keep chilli powder and black salt separately in a dish.

Mix together the roasted *hing* and ground roasted cumin seeds and keep aside.

Put the mixture of coriander, potato, cucumber, onion and salt onto individual plates.

Top it with a handful of *sev* and puffed rice.

Sprinkle with lemon juice, a couple of pinches of *hing* and ground cumin seeds, chilli powder and black salt according to taste and mix.

For a sweet and sour taste put a spoonful of tamarind chutney on top. It is a very tasty and fresh starter or snack.

BREAD CUTLETS

Ingredients

3 medium potatoes (boiled, peeled and cut into very small pieces)
1 cup peas (boiled and crushed)
8 slices white bread
2 tsp cumin seeds
1 tsp coriander powder
½ tsp chilli powder
½ tsp salt
3 tbs oil (for the preparation of the filling)
8–9 sprigs of green coriander (cleaned, chopped and washed)
oil for shallow frying
water in a broad bowl (for dipping the bread)

METHOD

Filling

Heat the oil in a frying pan. Add the cumin seeds and coriander powder and fry for a couple of seconds.

Add the potatoes, peas, salt and chilli powder, and keep frying for approximately 4–5 minutes on medium heat.

Lower the heat and fry for a further 5 minutes. Mix in the green coriander and keep this mixture aside.

Cutlets

Take a slice of bread, soak it in water, take it out immediately and squeeze the water out with your palm.

Put a spoonful of filling on the slice of bread, fold it in half carefully and shallow-fry it on medium heat on one side until it is golden brown. Turn it over and fry it again until it is golden brown.

Fry all the pieces in the same way. Take them out and place in a container lined with kitchen paper.

Serve them hot with chutney, tomato sauce and pickle. They are delicious.

CHICKPEA CHAAT
(*SAFED* OR *KABULI CHANA CHAAT*)

Ingredients

2 cups boiled chickpeas
1 medium onion (chopped into small, fine pieces)
2 lemons (cut in half)
3 tsp cumin seeds (dry roasted and crushed)
1 tsp salt (if using canned chickpeas use ¼ teaspoon salt)
1 tsp chilli powder or 3 green chillies (chopped into small fine pieces)

METHOD

Add the salt (according to taste) to the boiled chickpeas and mix together.

Keep the other ingredients on a separate plate.

While serving, sprinkle a pinch of crushed roasted cumin seeds, chopped green chillies or chilli powder, chopped onion and a dash of lemon juice on each plate and mix.

This snack is completely oil-free, healthy and delicious.

You can make similar snacks using black gram or any other whole beans such as moong beans and black-eyed beans.

POTATO CHAAT (*AALOO CHAAT*)

Ingredients

4 medium potatoes (boiled, peeled and cut into small, thin pieces)
1 small onion (peeled and chopped)
2 green chillies (washed and finely chopped) or ¼ tsp chilli powder
2 lemons (juice)
1 tsp salt
3 tsp roasted and ground cumin seeds
pinch of hing *(roasted)*

METHOD

Place all the ingredients in a glass or steel bowl and mix well. Sprinkle with the roasted *hing* and cumin seeds.

If you want a milder *chaat*, you can use sweet prune and tamarind chutney instead of chillies. Serve on plates with cocktail sticks.

SPICY FRUIT CHAAT
(*PHAL KI CHAAT*)

Ingredients

1 ripe banana
2 Golden Delicious apples
1 pear
1 guava
1 large bunch grapes (seedless)
2–3 plums
1 tsp cumin seeds (roasted and ground)
¼ teaspoon salt
½ lemon (juice)

METHOD

Cut all the fruit into small pieces (except the grapes, which can be halved or left whole). Put all the ingredients, including the spices and lemon juice, into a large bowl and mix together. This fruit salad is delicious and nutritious.

SPICY SOYA BEAN CHAAT

Ingredients

250 g soya beans (soaked overnight)
½ lemon (juice – according to taste)
1 onion (finely chopped)
2–3 green chillies (washed and finely chopped)
4–5 sprigs coriander (washed and chopped)
½ tsp salt (according to taste)
1 litre water (approx.)

METHOD

Boil the soya beans until tender. Drain off the water, and let the beans cool. Mix the beans with the chopped onion, green coriander, salt and lemon juice. It is a good relish and can also be served with vegetable salad.

FRIED SPICY CHICKPEAS (*MASAALA CHANA*)

Ingredients

2 cups chickpeas (soaked overnight and boiled) or 450 g can boiled chickpeas
1 medium onion (chopped, for frying)
1 medium onion (finely chopped, for sprinkling)
2.5 cm ginger (peeled, washed and chopped)
2 green chillies (washed and chopped, remove the stalks)
1 tsp cumin seeds
1 tsp turmeric powder
2 tsp coriander powder
1 tsp salt (according to taste)
3 tsp mango powder or juice of 1 lemon (according to taste)
2–3 tbs oil

METHOD

Heat the oil and fry the chopped onions until golden brown. Add the cumin seeds, turmeric powder and coriander powder and fry for a couple of seconds. Add the ginger and green chillies.

Next add the chickpeas and the salt and fry for 10–15 minutes on medium heat. Add the mango powder or lemon juice, mix well and cook for another 2–3 minutes.

Sprinkle with chopped onion (5–6 pieces per dish) and green coriander and serve hot.

PAAPAD

Paapad can be used as a light starter or just as a snack. You can buy them in Asian shops and some superstores. They are made of lentils or rice. Hot *paapad* contain a large amount of black pepper and spices. Generally rice *paapad* are not very hot. You can also buy mild lentil *paapad*. Rice *paapad* are always fried, but lentil *paapad* can be roasted or fried (known as *pappadoms* in south India). In my recipes I have only used lentil *paapad*.

FRIED PAAPAD

4–5 paapad *(cut each of them into four pieces)*
small quantity of oil for deep frying (use a very small frying pan)

METHOD

Heat the oil in a small frying pan, then fry the *paapad* one by one on both sides for a short time. Just a couple of seconds is enough for each piece. As soon as it puffs up, take it out with tongs. Avoid overheating the oil or overcooking the *paapad*. They should be golden in colour when fried. Avoid over or under-frying or they will lose their taste.

Line a serving bowl or a plate with kitchen paper and arrange all the pieces carefully, one by one, so they don't break.

Paapad can be served as a snack or a side dish (especially with rice), with mango chutney, green salad and pickle.

You will find many varieties of *paapad* in Asian shops. There are also many types of fritters, made of lentils, rice and arrowroot. These all need to be fried in hot oil.

DRY ROASTED PAAPAD

5–6 paapad

METHOD

You can roast the *paapad* either on an open flame or in a microwave.

Open-flame roasting

If you are roasting on an open flame cook one *paapad* at a time. Keep turning the *paapad* over – 3–4 times – very quickly with tongs (on a medium flame) until it becomes a little brown, spotty and crunchy. One *paapad* takes about a minute to roast.

Microwave roasting

Put one *paapad* on a piece of kitchen paper on high temperature for about 1 minute. Turn it over and cook for 1 minute (approximately), then remove it. Repeat with the remaining *paapad*.

You can serve them as a side dish, with rice, *daal* and *chapaatis*.

POTATO TIKKI (*AALOO TIKKI*)

Ingredients

1 cup peas (boiled and mashed)
4 medium potatoes (boiled, peeled and mashed)
3 slices white bread (make breadcrumbs in the grinder)
2.5 cm ginger (peeled and chopped)
7–8 sprigs green coriander (washed and chopped into small pieces)
2 tsp cumin seeds
¼ tsp hing (optional)
1 tsp chilli powder (you can use more if you want it hot)
1 tsp salt
2 tbs oil for the mixture
oil for shallow frying

METHOD

Mix together the peas, potatoes, ginger, chopped coriander, cumin seeds, *hing*, chilli powder, salt and breadcrumbs. Add 2 tablespoons of oil and knead the mixture until it is smooth like dough. It will make about 12 *tikkis*.

Divide this mixture into 12 portions and make each of them round with your hand. Gradually flatten them with your palm in the centre until approximately 7 cm in diameter and ½ cm or less thick.

Use a griddle and shallow-fry them in oil on medium heat until they are crunchy and dark golden brown on both sides. (Keep turning at regular intervals.)

If your griddle is big enough, you can fry 3 or 4 *tikkis* at a time. When you fry them, use oil liberally on both sides.

Serve them with tomato ketchup or herb chutney, and sweet and sour tamarind chutney.

SAMOSAS

Samosas are a very popular snack in north India. They can be used at cocktail parties, tea parties or as a starter or afternoon snack. They can be made in different sizes – very small, medium and large. Very small ones are good as cocktail snacks.

They are made of plain white flour, with vegetable filling. My favourite filling is made with potatoes, peas, and green coriander.

Ingredients
Makes approximately 20 samosas

Pastry

3 cups plain white flour
½ cup oil for kneading the flour
1 tsp salt
1 cup lukewarm water (add gradually)
oil for frying

Filling

4 medium potatoes (boiled and chopped into very small pieces)
1 cup peas (boiled and lightly mashed)
2 tbs oil
2 tsp cumin seeds
1 tsp salt (according to taste)
1 tsp chilli powder (reduce quantity according to taste)
3 tsp coriander powder
3 tsp mango powder
1 tsp paprika powder
1 tsp garam masaala
pinch of hing (optional)
½ cup green coriander (washed and chopped)

METHOD

Pastry

Mix together the flour, salt and oil in a bowl. Add the water gradually to make a dough. Knead the dough until it is soft and pliable. Leave aside for 10–15 minutes.

Meanwhile make the filling for the samosas.

Filling

Heat the oil in a frying pan. Add the *hing*, cumin seeds, coriander powder, paprika powder and garam masaala and fry for couple of seconds.

Add the potatoes, peas, salt and chilli powder. Mix together, and fry until the mixture is golden in colour. Add the mango powder, mix well and remove from the heat. Mix in the chopped coriander.

Pastry rolling and making samosas with the filling

Divide the pastry into 10–12 pieces, roll each piece into a circle approximately 8–9 cm in diameter and cut in half.

Fold the half circle and seal it with a drop of water (spread it with your finger). It will become cone-shaped.

Fill the cone with a tablespoon of filling, and seal the top exactly as you sealed the sides, with a drop of water.

One pastry piece will make two samosas. When all the samosas are made, cover them on a tray with a tea towel.

Heat the oil in a wok or *karahi* (Indian equivalent of a wok) and fry the samosas (4–5 at a time, depending on the size of wok or *karahi*) until they become golden brown.

Serve them at teatime or as a starter, with coriander chutney, tamarind chutney or tomato sauce.

Figure 1:

Pastry Rolling and Making Samosas

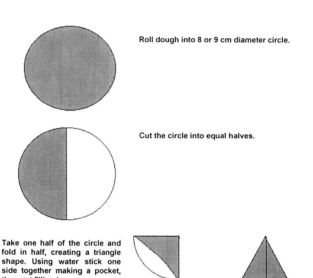

Roll dough into 8 or 9 cm diameter circle.

Cut the circle into equal halves.

Take one half of the circle and fold in half, creating a triangle shape. Using water stick one side together making a pocket, then put filling in.

Finally, after putting filling in (not over-stuffing the samosas), stick the third side together using water as before.

SPICY FRIED BREAD
(BREAD *PAKORAS*)

Ingredients

2 cups gram flour
1 cup water (approx.)
4 slices bread (cut in half or quarters)
oil for deep frying
pinch of hing
1 tsp cumin seeds
¼ tsp chilli powder
2 tsp coriander powder
½ tsp salt
7–8 tender sprigs of green coriander (cleaned, chopped and washed)

METHOD

Batter

Mix together the gram flour, salt, *hing*, cumin seeds, chilli powder and coriander powder in a bowl. Add the water gradually to make a batter just as for *pakoras*. It should have the consistency of medium-thick soup.

Add a few drops of oil to the batter – it helps to make the bread crispy. Add the chopped coriander and mix well.

Frying

Heat the oil in a *karahi* (wok) or deep frying pan. Take the bread pieces one by one and coat them with the batter. Fry them on medium heat until they are golden brown on both sides.

Put them in a dish lined with kitchen paper. Fry all the pieces in the same way. Serve them hot with sweet and sour tamarind chutney, green coriander chutney or tomato ketchup.

SPICY NAMAKPAARE

These are made with plain white flour, salt, cumin seeds and black peppercorns. They are a very tasty snack to have with drinks or with a cup of tea.

Ingredients

2 cups plain white flour
1 tsp salt
2 tsp cumin seeds
¼ cup black peppercorns (washed) – optional
½ cup oil
1 cup lukewarm water
oil for frying

METHOD

Pastry

Place the dry ingredients (except the peppercorns) in a mixing bowl. Add the water gradually to form a dough, and knead until smooth and soft.

Rolling and making *namakpaare*

Divide the dough into 4 portions. Roll each of them separately into flat circles approximately 13–14 cm in diameter and ½ cm thick.

Cut them into diamond shapes – see diagram below (2.5 cm long, 1 cm wide), prick them each in 2–3 places with a fork, stick 1–2 peppercorns in the centre of each diamond and keep them aside.

Frying

Heat the oil in a *karahi* or deep frying pan. When the oil is quite hot, turn the heat down to medium and fry 15–20 diamonds at a time, until golden in colour on both sides.

When all the diamonds have been fried, transfer them to a large plate lined with kitchen paper and leave to cool. Store them in an airtight container.

Serve them as a snack on their own or with mango pickle, sweet chutney or coriander chutney.

You can also make them in larger round shapes called *mathees*. (*Mathees* are approximately 7.5 cm in diameter.) *Mathees* can be kept for several days and are an excellent snack at teatime.

Diamond Shapes

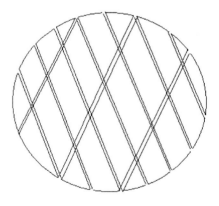

SPROUTED MOONG BEANS

You can sprout the beans yourself. Soak the whole beans overnight. Next day, drain off the water, put them in a piece of cheesecloth while still moist, and tie them loosely, or put them in a glass jar or bottle, cover its mouth with a piece of cloth and tie the cloth with string or an elastic band. Keep them moist by sprinkling some water over them from time to time every day. Shake them every day. Within 3–4 days you will see the sprouts. If you want them bigger you can leave them for a couple more days. You can also buy them in the market.

Ingredients

25 g bean sprouts
1 medium onion (peeled and chopped)
2 green chillies (washed and chopped)
1 tbs ginger (washed, peeled and grated)
1 lime or lemon (juice – according to taste)
½ tsp salt

METHOD

Steam the sprouted beans until they are tender, drain the water and add the onion, chillies, ginger, lemon and salt and mix.

This is a very healthy and nourishing snack. Whole gram or chickpeas can be prepared in the same way.

VEGETABLE PAKORAS

Ingredients

Batter

*4 cups gram flour (*besan*)*
2 cups water (you may need more water, the batter should have the consistency of a thin coating sauce)
$\frac{1}{2}$ tsp oil (to be added to the mixture)
2 tsp cumin seeds
pinch of bicarbonate of soda
$1\frac{1}{2}$ tsp salt
1 tsp chilli powder
2 tsp coriander powder
6–7 sprigs of green coriander (washed and chopped into small pieces)
oil for deep-frying

Vegetables for pakoras

(The following sizes are just a suggestion and may be varied)

2 medium potatoes (peeled, washed and sliced into rounds, approx. $\frac{1}{4}$ cm thick)
1 aubergine (washed and cut thinly lengthwise – approx. $\frac{1}{4}$ cm thick)
1 small cauliflower (cut the florets into pieces approx. 4 or 5 cm long and about 1.5 cm thick and wash)
1 onion (peeled and cut into thin rounds or chopped into small pieces)
5–6 leaves of spinach (washed)

Keep all the vegetables aside until they are almost dry.

METHOD

Batter

Place the gram flour, cumin seeds, bicarbonate of soda (just a pinch), salt, chilli powder and coriander powder in a large bowl. Mix them together with a fork or spoon. Mix in the chopped coriander and oil.

Add the water gradually in small amounts, mixing well. The batter should have a coating consistency. Leave it for 5–10 minutes, beat it again, then use it for making the *pakoras*.

Frying

Heat the oil in a wok or a deep frying pan. There should be enough oil for deep-frying.

Take 5–6 pieces of potato. Dip each piece in the batter until fully covered and fry them together. When these pieces are light-golden brown in colour, take them out and place them in a dish lined with kitchen paper.

Continue in this way until all the pieces have been fried.

Fry the aubergine pieces, then the cauliflower pieces, in the same way until they become golden brown.

(If you want to make cauliflower *pakoras* tastier and crispier, just fry them lightly, remove from the wok and let them cool. Now press them gently with kitchen paper and your palm and refry them for a while until they become golden brown.)

Onion pakoras

Onions can be cut into rings or chopped into small pieces. If cut into rings, use the same method as for the other vegetables.

If using chopped onions mix them into the batter, spoon the mixture into the hot oil (one spoonful for each *pakora*) and fry until golden brown. You may have to spoon the mixture a few times until the *karahi* has enough *pakoras* for cooking.

Spinach pakoras

Some people are particularly fond of spinach *pakoras* because they are very crisp. Take 5–6 leaves of spinach with a little part of the stem and wash them well. If they are too big, cut them in half. Dip them in the batter one by one until fully covered and fry until golden in colour. They are very tasty.

Serve the vegetable *pakoras* with coriander and mint chutney, mango pickle, ketchup and salad.

Salads

MIXED VEGETABLE SALAD

Salads

Spicy Salads

The following salads are delicious and easy to prepare. Carrots, radish, leeks, steamed asparagus and cucumber can be served with a dip as a starter.

A *kachoomar* is a grated salad and *kutra* is a finely cut salad.

BEETROOT SALAD
(*CHUKANDER SALAAD*)

Ingredients

2 beetroots (washed and thinly sliced)
¼ tsp salt
1 tbs lemon juice

METHOD

Cut the beetroot into thin rounds and boil in salted water until soft. Cool it then serve it as a salad. Add a pinch of salt and a dash of lemon. It is a good source of vitamin C and iron.

CARROT AND HORSERADISH SALAD (*GAJAR MOOLI KACHOOMAR*)

Ingredients

3–4 carrots (washed, scraped and grated)
1 horseradish (washed, scraped and grated – you can buy horseradish at an Indian grocer's)
¼ lemon (juice)
2 tsp mustard seeds
1 tsp oil
¼ tsp salt (according to taste)
1 green chilli (finely chopped)

METHOD

Mix all the ingredients together in a bowl except the mustard seeds and oil.

Heat the oil in a small frying pan. When it is hot add the mustard seeds, and when they start crackling add the oil and seeds to the salad and mix well. This delicious salad is a good accompaniment with any lunch or dinner.

MIXED VEGETABLE SALAD
(*MILI JULI SABZI SALAAD*)

Ingredients

1 cucumber (washed and sliced into thin rounds)
2–3 carrots (washed and sliced into thin rounds)
1 stick of celery (washed and cut into thin rounds)
1 onion (peeled and cut into thin rounds)
2 large peppers – different colours (washed and sliced thinly into rounds – discard the stalks and seeds)
1 lettuce (washed and dried)
1 tbs dry roasted mustard seeds (coarsely ground)
1 tbs English mustard
¼ tbs lemon juice
1 tsp ground black pepper
1 tsp olive oil
½ tsp salt

METHOD

Wash the lettuce thoroughly. Dry it gently with a tea towel, then tear roughly with your hand into small pieces. (Do not use a knife as it discolours the lettuce.)

Mix together all the vegetables, spices, lemon juice and olive oil 5 minutes before serving.

Put all the mixed vegetables in the centre of the serving dish and decorate the sides with lettuce leaves.

MUSHROOM AND BROCCOLI SALAD

Ingredients

2 cloves garlic (crushed)
2–3 tomatoes (washed and sliced)
3–4 florets broccoli (washed, and steamed if desired)
3–4 mushrooms (washed and thinly sliced)
1 tbs dry roasted sunflower seeds.
3–4 green chillies (washed and cut into tiny pieces – these are
optional, or you can reduce the quantity)
½ tsp salt
1 tsp olive oil or any vegetable oil

METHOD

Liquidise the green chillies and salt together with a minimum amount of water, mix in the olive oil, and add the mixture to all the other salad items in a large bowl. Mix well together.

You can serve this as a side dish with any type of lunch or dinner.

PASTA SALAD

Pasta salad is very nourishing and filling. It is full of protein and vitamins. Pasta is made with flour and water and is considered a good source of carbohydrate and protein. It can provide a healthy main meal, which is low in fat.

Ingredients

2 cups pasta – any shape (not spaghetti)
1 medium onion (chopped into small pieces)
2 medium tomatoes (washed and chopped into small pieces)
1 pepper – any colour (washed and thinly sliced)
3–4 button mushrooms (washed and thinly sliced)
¼ tsp salt
1 tbs mustard seeds (roasted and ground)
1 tsp olive oil
1 green chilli (washed and thinly slice – optional) or black pepper (ground)

METHOD

Boil the pasta with the olive oil and salt as per instructions on the packet. When it is ready, put it in a colander and wash it with cold water.

Put all the vegetables in a bowl and mix with the pasta. Sprinkle the pasta with olive oil, ground mustard, salt and green chilli or black pepper. Mix all the ingredients well and serve as a side dish.

VEGETABLE AND SUNFLOWER SEED SALAD

Ingredients

¼ *small red cabbage (washed and very thinly sliced)*
1–2 green chillies (washed and cut into small pieces)
1 yellow pepper (washed and thinly sliced lengthwise)
1 tbs sunflower seeds (roasted)
pinch of salt
1 tsp lemon juice

METHOD

Mix all the ingredients together in a glass bowl. Serve after 5–10 minutes.

VEGETABLE PASTA SALAD

Ingredients

100 g macaroni
2 tomatoes (washed and chopped into small pieces)
1 cup frozen or fresh peas (if using fresh peas, boil them first)
½ cup carrots (washed and thinly sliced)
1 red or green pepper (washed and sliced thinly lengthwise)
2 medium onions (sliced into small pieces)
1 green chilli (washed and chopped into small pieces) or black pepper (according to taste)
½ tsp salt
2 tbs olive oil

METHOD

First boil the macaroni for 6–10 minutes until it becomes tender but not broken. Before boiling add some salt and a teaspoon of olive oil (or any cooking oil) to the water.

Put 2–3 tablespoons of oil in a wok or frying pan. When the oil is hot, add the onion and green chilli and fry until the onions are pale-golden brown.

Add the tomatoes, fry them for about 2 minutes, then add the pepper and peas. Fry the vegetables until they are completely tender, then add the salt.

Put the boiled macaroni in a colander, wash once with cold water (to remove the starch from the boiled macaroni) and add it to the fried vegetables. Mix together and cover.

Simmer for a few minutes, stirring a couple of times. Serve hot for main meals or cold for salads.

FRESH GREEN MANGO KACHOOMAR

Ingredients

1 medium, hard, raw green mango (washed, peeled and grated, discard the stone)
2–3 green chillies (washed and chopped into small pieces, discard the stems)
4–5 sprigs of mint (use the leaves and discard the stems, wash them and chop)
1 tsp salt
½ tsp hing
1 tsp cumin seeds (roasted)

METHOD

Mix together all the spices, grated mango and mint. This fresh mango salad is a good accompaniment to any meal.

MIXED KUTRA (*MILA JULA KUTRA*)

Ingredients

1 cucumber (washed and chopped into small pieces)
2 tomatoes (washed and chopped into small pieces)
1 red pepper (washed and chopped into small pieces)
2 carrots (washed and chopped into small pieces)
1 medium onion (peeled and chopped into small pieces)
2 green chillies (washed and chopped, do not remove seeds – you can
reduce/increase the quantity to suit your taste)
¼ lemon (juice)
¼ tsp salt (according to taste)
1 clove garlic (peeled and chopped into fine pieces)

METHOD

If you do not like green chillies you can add a little ground black pepper instead.

Place all the ingredients and vegetables in a bowl and mix them well. Mix in a few drops of olive oil. This salad can be served with rice, *daal* and *chapaatis*.

Vegetable Dishes

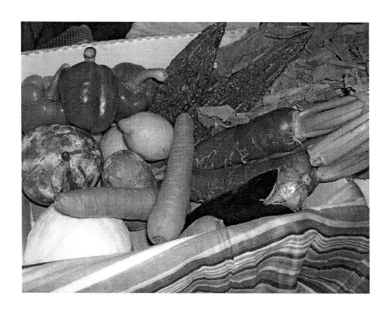

FRESH VEGETABLES

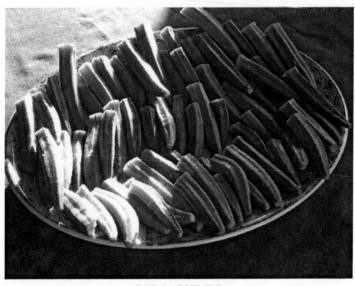

OKRA (*BHINDI*)

Vegetable Dishes

Vegetable Dishes

AUBERGINES AND POTATOES (*BAINGAN AALOO*)

There are several methods of cooking aubergines, some of which I have described below. In this recipe you can use any type of aubergine because all have a similar taste. You can buy them from greengrocers in different sizes and varieties – small, large, blue, black or white.

Ingredients

1–2 large aubergines or 5–6 small aubergines (cut each in half, then cut lengthwise, approx. ½ cm thick, discard the stems or tails and wash)
2–3 medium potatoes (peeled, washed and cut into medium pieces)
2–3 green chillies (washed and cut into very small pieces – optional)
2.5 cm green ginger (scraped, washed and finely chopped)
1 medium onion (peeled and thinly cut)
pinch of hing *(optional)*
1 tsp cumin seeds
1 tsp salt
2–3 tsp coriander powder
1 tsp turmeric powder
2 tsp mango powder (for a tangy taste) or a dash of lemon
3–4 tbs of oil

METHOD

Put the oil into the frying pan. When it is hot, add the onion, *hing* and ginger. Fry until the onion is lightly golden, then add the cumin seeds, coriander powder and turmeric powder.

Add the potatoes and fry them for 3–4 minutes, then add the aubergines, green chillies and salt. Mix together and cover. Simmer the potatoes and aubergines on a medium heat until both are well cooked, stirring occasionally. You can add some water if necessary.

There should be no liquid – or very little liquid – left when fully cooked. (The vegetables should be almost dry.) Sprinkle with mango powder or a dash of lemon and mix well. Cover for a few minutes. You can serve it with all types of Indian bread, also with bread rolls or rice.

BEAN SPROUTS AND MIXED VEGETABLES
(*LUNGI AUR MILI JULI SAZBI*)

Ingredients

1 pack of bean sprouts
2–3 carrots (washed and finely chopped)
10–12 runner beans (washed and cut into small pieces)
2–3 green chillies (washed and finely chopped – optional)
2.5 cm ginger (scraped, washed and finely cut)
1 onion (sliced)
1 medium potato (peeled, washed and cut into small pieces)
1 red pepper (washed and cut into small pieces)
1 tsp cumin seeds
1 tsp garam masaala
¼ tsp turmeric powder
½ tsp salt
3–4 tbs oil
4–5 tbs water (if necessary)

METHOD

Fry the onion in the oil until it is golden brown. Add the spices and fry for a couple of seconds.

Add the vegetables, green chillies, ginger and salt, and fry them for a couple of minutes. If necessary, add 4–5 tablespoons of water. Cover them and cook for 5–10 minutes until all the vegetables are soft and tender and all the liquid has evaporated.

This dish can be served with *chapaatis* or *paraathas*.

BOILED SWEET POTATOES
(*UBLI SHAKERKANDI*)

Ingredients

4 sweet potatoes
1 tbs vegan margarine
½ tsp salt
2 tsp black pepper
dash of lemon juice

METHOD

Boil the sweet potatoes until tender but firm.

Peel them, cut them into small pieces and mix in the margarine, salt and pepper and a dash of lemon juice. They are delicious.

BROCCOLI AND POTATOES (BROCCOLI *AALOO*)

Ingredients

500 g (approx.) broccoli (washed and cut into small pieces)
2–3 medium potatoes (washed and cut into small pieces)
1 medium onion (thinly sliced)
1–2 cloves garlic (peeled and sliced – optional)
1–2 green chillies (washed and chopped)
½ tsp salt
1 tsp cumin seeds
1–2 tsp coriander powder
1 tsp garam masaala
3 tbs oil
3–4 sprigs of green coriander (washed and chopped)
½ cup of water

METHOD

Heat the oil and fry the onion and garlic. When it is pale gold add the cumin seeds and other spices.

When the seeds start crackling, add the potato pieces, salt and green chillies. Add half a cup of water.

When they are half cooked, add the broccoli florets, cover, and keep cooking until both the vegetables are well cooked and tender. They should be almost dry when ready.

Garnish with green coriander and a pinch of garam masaala. Serve with any type of bread.

CABBAGE AND PEAS
(*BANDH GOBHI MATAR*)

Ingredients

1 medium cabbage (washed and thinly sliced or shredded)
100 g peas (frozen or fresh)
2.5 cm ginger (washed, scraped and finely cut or grated)
2 green chillies (washed and chopped)
1 clove garlic (chopped – optional)
2–3 tbs oil
½ tsp salt (according to taste)
1 tsp cumin seeds
¼ tsp fenugreek seeds
2 tsp mustard seeds
1 tsp turmeric powder
2–3 tsp coriander powder
1 tsp mango powder

METHOD

Heat the oil in a frying pan. When it is hot enough, add the fenugreek (*methi*) mustard and cumin seeds.

When they start spluttering add the ginger and garlic and fry for a couple of seconds. Add the turmeric powder, coriander powder and peas, fry them for 2 minutes, then add the shredded cabbage, salt and green chillies.

Cover them and cook for approximately 15 minutes on medium heat until the cabbage and peas are soft and the water has evaporated. Keep stirring them every 2–3 minutes.

Finally add the mango powder (*amchoor*), mix well and keep covered for a couple of minutes. Serve with rice or bread.

Cabbage can also be used in the following recipes: cabbage and potatoes; cabbage and lentils; shredded and fried cabbage and cabbage *pakoras* or *bhajia*.

CARROTS AND PEAS
(*GAAJAR MATAR*)

Ingredients

500 g carrots (scraped, washed and cut into small pieces about ½ cm thick)
250 g peas (frozen or fresh)
2.5 cm ginger (peeled and chopped into very small pieces)
2–3 green chillies (washed and cut into small pieces)
pinch of hing – optional
1 tsp cumin seeds
½ tsp salt (according to taste)
2 tsp coriander powder
1 tsp turmeric powder
1 tsp mango powder (amchoor)
2–3 tbs cooking oil
1–2 tbs water (if necessary)

METHOD

Heat the oil in a frying pan. Add the *hing*, cumin seeds, coriander powder and ginger and fry for a couple of seconds.

Add the carrots, peas, green chillies and salt. Mix everything together well and cover. Cook until the carrots are tender, then add the mango powder, mix well and cover again (adding a little water if necessary).

The vegetables should become quite dry and tender. You can serve them with any type of bread.

COURGETTES (*TORI*)

Ingredients

900 g courgettes (peeled, washed and cut into small pieces or rings)
2.5 cm ginger (peeled, washed and chopped)
2 green chillies (washed and chopped – optional, or you can reduce the quantity)
juice of ¼ lemon (add when the vegetables are ready, according to taste)
1 tsp cumin seeds
pinch of hing
½ tsp salt
1 tsp turmeric powder
2 tsp coriander powder
2 tbs cooking oil

METHOD

Heat the oil in a saucepan. Add the *hing,* cumin seeds, turmeric and coriander powder and ginger and fry for a couple of seconds.

Add the courgettes, green chillies and salt and cook them on medium heat until well cooked and semi-liquid.

Add a few drops of fresh lemon juice. Mix everything together well and serve with bread or rice.

DEEP-FRIED AUBERGINES
(*TALAE BAINGAN*)

Ingredients

2 aubergines (large)
½ tsp salt
½ tsp chilli powder
1 tsp garam masaala (mixture of finely ground cloves, black cardamom, cinnamon and black pepper)
8–10 sprigs of green coriander (chopped, washed and dried with kitchen paper or a tea towel)
oil for deep-frying (use a wok or frying pan for frying – it should be deep enough for frying vegetables)

METHOD

Wash the aubergines. Cut them into rounds ½–1 cm thick. Discard the stems.

Heat the oil to frying temperature. Turn the heat down and add the aubergine rounds carefully (because hot oil might splash). You can add 10–12 rounds or more at a time depending on the quantity of oil and the size of the wok or *karahi*.

When all the pieces have been fried, arrange them in a serving dish lined with kitchen paper to soak up excess oil. Sprinkle spices over them and serve as a snack or with meals.

Serve them with *paraathas, chapaatis* or sliced bread.

DEEP-FRIED MASAALA AUBERGINE (*TALAE MASAALA BAINGAN*)

Ingredients

2 aubergines (washed and cut into rounds ½–1 cm thick)
1 tsp cumin seeds
¼ tsp salt
½ tsp turmeric powder
¼ tsp chilli powder
½ tsp garam masaala
oil for deep-frying
3–4 tbs water

METHOD

Fry the aubergine pieces exactly as for deep-fried aubergine in the previous recipe, and keep them aside.

Put the oil in the frying pan, add the seeds and spices and fry for a couple of seconds on medium heat. Add the fried pieces of aubergine and salt. Add 3–4 tablespoons of water, mix well and cook for a couple of minutes. Keep covered.

When it is almost dry, serve with rice, *chapaatis*, *paraathas*, or *pooris*, or even with bread rolls, sliced bread or toast.

FRENCH BEANS AND POTATOES (*FRANS BEEN AALOO*)

Ingredients

500 g French beans, or any variety of green beans (topped and tailed, cut into small pieces approx. 2.5 cm, and washed)
2 medium potatoes (peeled, washed and cut into medium pieces)
1 medium onion (sliced thinly)
pinch of hing
1 tsp cumin seeds
½ tsp garam masaala
¾ tsp turmeric powder
2 tsp coriander powder
¼ tsp chilli powder (optional)
1 tsp salt
2.5 cm piece of ginger (peeled, washed and finely chopped)
8–9 sprigs of green coriander (washed and chopped)
3–4 tbs oil
3–4 tbs water

METHOD

Heat the oil in a deep-frying pan. Add the onion and fry until golden. Add the cumin seeds, garam masaala, turmeric and coriander powder and fry for a couple of minutes.

Add the potatoes and ginger and fry for 2–3 minutes. Now add the beans, chilli powder and salt, cover, and cook on medium heat.

Keep stirring every 2–3 minutes until the beans and potatoes become tender.

If necessary you can add 3–4 tablespoons of water.

When ready, decorate with chopped coriander and serve with any type of bread.

GOURD (*GHIA*)

Ingredients

1 medium gourd (peeled, cut into small thin pieces, and washed)
2.5 cm ginger (peeled, washed and chopped)
1–2 green chillies (washed and chopped)
pinch of hing
1 tsp cumin seeds
1 tsp paprika
1 tsp turmeric powder
1–2 tsp coriander powder
½ tsp salt
2 tbs cooking oil
juice of ¼ lemon (according to taste)
½ cup water (if needed)

METHOD

Heat the oil in a saucepan and add the *hing*, ginger, cumin seeds and spices. Fry for a couple of seconds and add the sliced gourd and green chillies.

Cook on a medium heat until it is fairly soft and mushy.

It should be semi-liquid. It cooks in its own juice, but you can add a little water if necessary to make it tender.

Add the chopped green coriander and lemon juice and mix. Serve with *chapaatis, paraathas* or *pooris*.

GOURD KOFTAS IN MASAALA SAUCE (*GHIA KOFTE*)

Ingredients

Koftas

1 medium round or long gourd (washed, peeled and grated)
1 cup gram daal *(*chana daal, *soaked overnight, drain the water before use)*
*1 cup gram flour (*besan*)*
2.5 cm ginger (peeled, washed and grated)
1 green chilli (washed and chopped)
pinch of hing
1 tsp cumin seeds
2 tsp coriander powder
1 tsp garam masaala
½ tsp salt
oil for deep-frying koftas

Kofta masaala sauce

1 medium onion (cut into medium pieces)
2 tomatoes (washed and cut into small pieces)
1 tbs tomato puree
2.5 cm ginger (peeled, washed and cut)
pinch of hing
1 tsp cumin seeds
1 tsp turmeric powder
¼ tsp chilli powder (according to taste, optional)
2 tsp coriander powder
1 tsp paprika
½ tsp salt

2 tsp plain white flour or cornflour
1 tbs dried fenugreek leaves
2–3 tbs cooking oil
3 cups water (approx.)

METHOD

Koftas

Steam the grated gourd for 5–7 minutes and, when tender, drain the water and keep the gourd aside.

Using a liquidiser, make a paste with the gram *daal* (*chana daal*), grated ginger and chopped green chilli with a minimum amount of water.

Make a batter for the koftas with the liquidised paste, gram flour (*besan*), *hing*, cumin seeds, green chilli, coriander powder, garam masaala and salt. Squeeze the steamed gourd, discard the water, and add to the other ingredients. Mix well together.

Make 15–16 koftas (round balls approx. 2 cm diameter rolled by hand – they should be firm) and keep them aside.

Now heat the oil in a wok and fry the koftas until golden brown, then remove them and keep in a bowl.

Masaala sauce

Using a liquidiser make a medium-thick paste with the onion, ginger, tomato and a little water.

Heat the oil in a saucepan and fry this paste with the cumin seeds and the turmeric, chilli, coriander and paprika powder until golden. Add the tomato purée and dried fenugreek leaves.

When it is light brown, add the plain white flour or cornflour and fry for a couple of minutes. Add 3 cups of water and the salt. Simmer for 10–15 minutes.

Add the koftas and simmer for approximately 5–6 minutes until they are soft.

Serve with rice and/or *chapaatis*.

KOHLRABI (*GAANTH GOBHI*)

Ingredients

5–6 medium kohlrabies
2.5 cm ginger (peeled, washed and chopped)
2–3 green chillies (washed and chopped into small pieces)
pinch of hing
1 tsp cumin seeds
½ tsp fenugreek seeds
1 tsp turmeric powder
2 tsp coriander powder
½ tsp garam masaala
1 tsp paprika
½ tsp salt (according to taste)
5–6 sprigs of coriander (washed and chopped)
2–3 tbs oil (approx.)
1 tbs lemon juice (optional)
½ cup water (if needed)

METHOD

Peel and cut the kohlrabies into small pieces about 2.5 cm long and ½ cm thick, keeping the leaves separate, whole or slightly chopped. Wash all of them thoroughly.

Heat the oil in a frying pan. Add the *hing*, ginger, cumin and fenugreek seeds, and the turmeric, coriander and paprika powder. Fry for a couple of seconds, then add the kohlrabi pieces, leaves, green chillies and salt. Mix well.

Cook for 15–20 minutes on medium heat until tender and well cooked (using a little water if required).

Just before serving, sprinkle with chopped coriander and lemon juice. Serve with any kind of bread or rice.

LEEKS AND POTATOES
(HARAA PIAZ AUR AALOO)

Ingredients

3–4 leeks (washed and thinly sliced into pieces 2.5 cm in length) or
8–9 spring onions
2–3 medium potatoes (peeled, washed and cut into medium pieces)
2–3 green chillies (washed and chopped)
1 tsp cumin seeds
1 tsp turmeric powder
1 tsp coriander powder
½ tsp salt (according to taste)
2–3 tbs oil

METHOD

Heat the oil in a frying pan. Add the cumin seeds, turmeric and coriander powder, then the potatoes, and fry them until pale gold. Keep stirring every 2–3 minutes.

Add the leeks, chopped green chillies and salt, mix well and cover. Cook on a low heat until all the vegetables are soft and tender. Add a little water if the potatoes are not soft enough.

When most of the water has evaporated, take off the lid and keep cooking until dry. Serve with any kind of bread or rice.

MARROW (*PHOOT*)

Ingredients

2 medium marrows (peeled, washed and cut into medium pieces)
1 medium onion (peeled and chopped)
1 tomato (washed and chopped)
2.5 cm ginger (peeled, washed and chopped)
2 green chillies (washed and chopped)
1 tsp cumin seeds
1 tsp turmeric powder
1 tsp coriander powder
½ tsp salt (according to taste)
1 tsp lemon juice (optional)
2 tbs oil
7–8 sprigs of coriander (washed and chopped)

METHOD

Heat the oil in a saucepan and fry the onion until pale gold.

Gradually add the cumin seeds, turmeric and coriander powder and ginger and fry for a couple of seconds. Add the chopped tomatoes and continue to fry until the tomatoes are quite soft.

Mix in the marrow pieces, green chillies and salt. Cover and cook on a medium heat for approximately 10–15 minutes. It will cook in its own juices – if it becomes too dry, add a little water. When it is soft and semi-liquid, remove from the heat. Sprinkle with the green coriander and lemon juice.

This dish can be served with any type of bread or rice.

You can make different dishes with marrow as with gourd, such as marrow koftas and marrow with *chana daal* (gram lentils).

MASAALA BITTER GOURD (*MASAALA KARELA*)

Bitter gourd, as the name suggests, is bitter but is considered good for the health. Smearing with salt, and leaving for at least one hour can reduce this bitter taste. You can obtain it from Asian grocery shops.

Ingredients

*10 bitter gourds (*karela*)*
2 tsp cumin seeds
10 tsp coriander powder
1 tsp turmeric powder
½ tsp red chilli powder
2 tsp mango powder
3–4 fennel seeds (optional)
3–4 tbs oil
3 tbs salt (approx. – for smearing only)

METHOD

Peel the bitter gourds (*karelas*) with a potato peeler, discard the tails and ends and make a slit lengthwise in the centre.

Smear salt inside and outside the peeled bitter gourds, and keep them aside for an hour or more.

Wash them thoroughly in cold water until most of the salt has been washed away.

Squeeze the water out thoroughly – press gently with your palm so that they are almost dry but not broken.

Mix all the spices together (except the *hing* and cumin and fennel seeds) and put one teaspoon of this filling in each of the slit bitter gourds. *Do not add any salt.*

Heat the oil in a frying pan and add the *hing*, cumin and fennel seeds and the stuffed bitter gourds.

Cover with a tight lid and cook on a low heat. Keep stirring them every couple of minutes, until they become soft and golden brown on all sides.

They cook in their own juice, but if necessary add 1–2 tablespoons of water. Try to keep them whole. When quite brown and tender, remove them from the heat. Serve them whole or cut into two to three pieces each with any type of bread.

MASAALA CAULIFLOWER (*BHUNA PHOOL GOBHI*)

Ingredients

1 medium cauliflower (cut into medium florets and washed)
1 medium onion (peeled and chopped)
2.5 cm ginger (peeled, washed and chopped)
2–3 green chillies (washed and chopped)
1 clove garlic (peeled and chopped)
1–2 tsp cumin seeds
1 tsp garam masaala
1 tsp turmeric powder
3 tsp coriander powder
½ tsp salt (according to taste)
7–8 sprigs chopped coriander
3–4 tbs oil
2 tbs water (if needed)

METHOD

Heat the oil in a frying pan. Fry the onion until golden.

Add the ginger, cumin seeds, turmeric and coriander powder and fry for a couple of seconds. Add the cauliflower, chopped garlic and green chillies and fry for a couple of seconds.

Add the salt and cover. Cook on a medium heat. When the contents are soft (add the water if needed), remove the lid and continue to cook until the water has evaporated and the florets look fried and dry.

Add the garam masaala and chopped coriander. Serve with any type of bread.

MASAALA DRY POTATOES
(*SOOKHE AALOO*)

Ingredients

5–6 medium potatoes
2 green chillies (washed and chopped)
1.5 cm ginger (peeled, washed and chopped)
pinch of hing
2 tsp cumin seeds
3 tsp coriander powder
1 tsp turmeric powder
2 tsp mango powder or 1 tbs lemon juice
3–4 tbs oil
1 tsp salt
2 tbs chopped coriander leaves
2 tbs water

METHOD

Boil the potatoes until tender but firm. Peel them and cut into medium pieces.

Heat the oil in a frying pan or wok. Add the *hing*, cumin seeds, coriander and turmeric powder. Fry for a couple of seconds and add the potatoes, chopped ginger, salt and mango powder or lemon juice and a little water if necessary.

Fry the potatoes on low heat until golden brown. Sprinkle with chopped coriander and serve with *parathaas* or *pooris*.

MASAALA GRILLED POTATOES (*BHUNE MASAALA AALOO*)

Ingredients

500 g new potatoes
2 tbs crushed mustard seeds
½ tsp salt
¼ tsp red chilli powder
2 tbs oil

METHOD

Boil the potatoes in a saucepan until they are soft, but not too soft or broken.

Peel them and cut them in half lengthwise. Arrange all these pieces in layers in a round or oval ovenproof dish.

Mix together the oil, salt, crushed mustard seeds and chilli powder in a small bowl. Spread this mixture over all the arranged pieces and shake them gently so that the spices cover all the layers.

Place the dish of potatoes under a hot grill and lower the heat to medium. Bake them for 5–7 minutes or until the potatoes are slightly brown.

Serve them with any type of bread or as a side dish.

MASAALA OKRA (*MASAALA BHINDI*)

Ingredients

*500 g okra (*bhindi*)*
2 medium onions (thinly sliced)
pinch of hing *powder*
½ tsp ajwain seeds (small seeds like cumin seeds)
1 tsp cumin seeds
¾ tsp turmeric powder
2 tsp coriander powder
¼ tsp chilli powder
1 tsp mango powder
½ tsp salt (according to taste)
2–3 tbs oil
5–6 sprigs of coriander (washed and chopped)
1–2 tbs water (if necessary)

METHOD

Wash the okra pods and wipe them with a tea towel, then cut them into small pieces (rounds), approximately 3–4 pieces per pod. Discard the stems.

Heat the oil in a frying pan. Add the sliced onions and fry for approximately 2–3 minutes.

Add the *hing*, ajwain seeds, cumin seeds, turmeric powder and coriander powder and fry for a couple of seconds. Then add the chopped okra, salt and chilli powder. Cover and cook on medium heat for 3–4 minutes. It usually cooks in its own juice, but if necessary add a little water.

Stir from time to time until the okra is soft. Add the mango powder and mix well. Remove the lid and stir gently until the okra pieces look roasted and almost dry, but not broken or mushy.

Decorate with the chopped coriander and serve with any type of bread.

MASAALA ONIONS AND BITTER GOURD
(*BHUNE PIAZ KARELA*)

Ingredients

*10 bitter gourds (*karela)
2–3 medium onions (peeled and sliced)
pinch of hing
2 tsp cumin seeds
2–3 tsp coriander powder
1 tsp turmeric powder
1 tsp red chilli powder
1 tsp paprika
2 tsp mango powder
2 tsp salt (for smearing only)
4–5 tbs oil or juice of 1 lemon

METHOD

Peel the bitter gourds and slice them into 6–7 small rounds, approximately 1 cm thick, depending on the size of each one.

Smear all the bitter gourd pieces with salt and keep them aside for an hour.

Wash them 4–5 times in cold water until the salt is washed away, then squeeze out all the water with your hands without crushing the pieces.

Heat the oil in a frying pan and add the *hing* and onion. Fry for a couple of minutes, then add the cumin seeds, coriander and turmeric powder, red chilli and paprika powder and bitter gourd pieces (but no salt).

Cover and cook on a low heat for 2–3 minutes.

Stir, cover and cook for a further for 2–3 minutes. Repeat until the bitter gourd pieces are soft and well fried. If necessary, add a tablespoon of water.

When they are soft, remove the lid and keep frying until the bitter gourd pieces are brown and the water has almost evaporated.

Sprinkle with mango powder or lemon juice and mix well. Serve with any type of bread.

MASAALA PEAS (*MASAALA MATTAR*)

Ingredients

500 g peas (fresh or frozen)
2.5 cm ginger
2 green chillies (washed and chopped)
1 tsp cumin seeds
1 tsp paprika
1 tsp turmeric powder
1 tsp coriander powder
1 tsp mango powder (add when vegetables are cooked and soft) or a few drops of lemon juice
1 tsp garam masaala
½ tsp salt
2 tbs oil
1 cup water (fresh peas may need some extra water to cook)

METHOD

Heat the oil in a frying pan. Add the cumin seeds and the paprika, turmeric and coriander powder. After a couple of seconds, add the ginger, peas and green chillies and mix well. Now add the water and salt and simmer until the peas are soft and well cooked.

Sprinkle with chopped coriander, mango powder or a dash of lemon. This dish can be served with any type of bread. It can be eaten alone or as a side dish or snack.

MASAALA POTATOES
(DUM MASAALA AALOO)

Ingredients

500 g new potatoes (semi-boiled, peeled and pricked with a fork)
1–2 green chillies (washed and chopped)
1 medium onion (peeled and chopped)
1 tbs tomato purée
*1 tbs dried fenugreek leaves (*kasuri methi*)*
pinch of hing
1 tsp cumin seeds
1 tsp salt (according to taste)
1 tsp paprika powder
1 tsp turmeric powder
1 tsp coriander powder
2 tbs corn meal flour or fine semolina
6 blanched almonds
½ cup coriander leaves (washed and chopped)
3–4 tbs oil (for masaala sauce)
3 cups water (approx.)
oil for deep-frying (for the potatoes)

METHOD

Frying the potatoes

Heat the oil in a *karahi* or wok and fry the potatoes on a medium heat until they are light brown in colour. Remove them and place them in a bowl lined with kitchen paper. Keep them aside.

Masaala sauce

Make the masaala paste in a liquidiser with the chopped onion, ginger, almonds and green chilli, using a little water.

Heat the oil in a saucepan and fry this paste. When it is well fried and golden in colour, add the tomato purée, paprika powder, coriander powder, fenugreek leaves, corn meal flour and salt and mix well. Fry for a couple of minutes and add the water to make the masaala sauce.

When it starts boiling, lower the heat to medium and simmer for 8–10 minutes. When it thickens, add the potatoes and simmer until they are soft but not broken. This dish should be semi-liquid.

Sprinkle with chopped coriander and serve with rice, *chapaatis* or any type of bread.

MASAALA POTATOES AND PEAS (*PIAZ WALE AALOO MATAR*)

Ingredients

250 g peas (fresh or frozen)
2 medium potatoes (peeled, washed and cut into medium pieces)
1 medium onion (peeled and chopped)
2.5 cm ginger (peeled, washed and chopped)
1 green chilli (washed and chopped)
1 tbs tomato purée
2 tsp cumin seeds
1 tbs dried fenugreek leaves
1 tsp paprika powder
1 tsp turmeric powder
1 tsp coriander powder
1 tsp salt (according to taste)
3–4 tbs oil
4 cups water (approx.)
2–3 tbs chopped coriander (washed and finely chopped)

METHOD

Make the masaala paste in a liquidiser with the onions, ginger and green chilli, using a little water. Ensure that the paste is as thick as possible.

Heat the oil in a saucepan and fry this paste. When it is well fried and pale gold in colour add the cumin seeds, tomato purée and paprika, turmeric, and coriander powder and fry for a couple of minutes.

Add the potatoes, peas and salt. Fry for another 2–3 minutes and then add the water.

Simmer for 10 minutes (approximately) on medium

heat. The consistency of the liquid should be that of thick soup, and the potatoes should be well cooked (if necessary simmer for a little longer).

Sprinkle with chopped coriander and serve with rice or any type of bread.

MASAALA MASHED AUBERGINE (*BAINGAN BHURTA*)

Ingredients

3–4 aubergines
2.5 cm ginger (peeled, washed and very finely chopped)
3 green chillies (washed and finely chopped – for a milder taste you could just add one)
2 onions (peeled and chopped)
2 tomatoes (washed and chopped)
1 tbs tomato purée
1 tsp cumin seeds
pinch of hing *(optional)*
1 tsp paprika powder
1 tsp turmeric powder
2–3 tsp coriander powder
1 tsp garam masaala
½ tsp salt (according to taste)
5–6 sprigs coriander (washed and chopped)
2–3 tbs of oil

METHOD

Wash the aubergines. Smear your palm with a few drops of oil and rub it all over the aubergines.

Slit the aubergines in the middle and put them under the grill on high until they give a pleasant roasting aroma, and the skin looks really black and charred on all sides (keep on turning).

Remove from the grill and keep aside to cool. (Instead of grilling the aubergines, you could roast them one by one on an open flame without slitting.)

Remove the charred peel with your hands, then wash the aubergines well in a deep dish, ensuring no part of the peel remains. Discard the stalks. Mash all the aubergines together and keep aside.

Heat the oil in a frying pan and add a little *hing*. Add the chopped onions and fry them for a couple of minutes. Add the cumin seeds, turmeric powder, coriander powder and garam masaala, and fry until the onions become golden brown.

Add the ginger and green chillies and fry for a couple of seconds, then add the tomatoes and the tomato purée and fry for 2–3 minutes.

Add the mashed aubergines and salt and fry until everything looks golden brown, stirring every 2–3 minutes. Serve with any type of bread or with rice.

MASAALA STEAMED BEANS (*PHALI BHAJI*)

Ingredients

450 g (approx.) dwarf beans (keep whole or cut in half, discard the stems and wash)
2.5 cm ginger (peeled, washed and finely chopped)
2 green chillies (washed and chopped – optional, or you can reduce the quantity)
2 tomatoes (washed and cut into medium pieces)
1 clove garlic (finely chopped)
1 tsp cumin seeds
1 tsp turmeric powder
2 tsp coriander powder.
1 tsp salt (according to taste)
2–3 tbs oil
water (approx. 3 cups)

METHOD

Boil the water (enough to cover the beans) in a saucepan. Add the beans and boil for about 5–6 minutes or until tender. Drain off the water and take out the beans. Keep them aside.

Heat the oil in a frying pan, add the cumin seeds, turmeric and coriander powder and fry for a couple of seconds.

Add the garlic, ginger and tomatoes and fry for a couple of minutes.

Add the beans, salt and green chillies, mix well, cover and cook for 5–6 minutes. Remove the cover and keep frying for a few minutes until tender and almost dry. Serve with any type of bread.

MASAALA TINDAS
(SPICY SMALL ROUND GOURDS)

Ingredients

10–12 tindas *(peeled, washed and cut into four pieces)*
2.5 cm ginger (peeled, washed and chopped)
2 green chillies (washed and chopped)
2 medium onions (peeled and chopped)
2 tbs tomato purée
pinch of hing
2 tsp cumin seeds
1 tsp paprika powder
1 tsp turmeric powder
2 tsp coriander powder
1 tsp salt
1 tsp mango powder
8–9 sprigs of coriander (washed and chopped)
2 cups (approx.) water (add gradually)
4 tbs oil

METHOD

Heat the oil in a saucepan and fry the onion until golden brown. Gradually add the *hing*, cumin seeds, paprika and turmeric powder and tomato purée. Fry for a couple of seconds.

Add the chopped *tindas*, ginger, green chillies and salt. Cover and cook on a medium heat for approximately 5 minutes.

Stir the *tindas* and add 1 cup of water, cover and cook until the pieces of *tinda* are soft. Add more water if necessary.

When the vegetables are soft and well cooked add the mango powder, stir and cover for a couple of minutes. Sprinkle with chopped coriander and serve with any type of bread.

MASAALA STUFFED TINDAS –
TINY GOURDS
(BHARWAN TINDE)

Tindas are small round gourds. You can buy them in any Asian grocery shop (generally in winter).

Ingredients

Masaala sauce for stuffed tindas

10–12 tindas *(peeled, washed and cut through in the centre like a cross, but do not separate the pieces)*
2.5 cm ginger (peeled, washed and chopped)
1 green chilli (washed and chopped)
1 medium onion (peeled and chopped into small pieces)
1 tomato (chopped)
2 tsp dried fenugreek leaves (kasuri methi – *you can buy packets in an Indian grocer's)*
2 tsp cumin seeds
pinch of hing *(optional)*
1 tsp turmeric powder
1–2 tsp paprika powder
3 tsp coriander powder
½ tsp garam masaala
½ tsp salt (according to taste)
1 tbs cornflour
3 cups water
3–4 tbs oil

Filling for tindas

1 tsp cumin seeds
½ tsp turmeric powder

3 tsp coriander powder
1 tsp mango powder
¼ tsp chilli powder
½ tsp salt
3 tbs oil
2–3 tbs water

METHOD

Masaala sauce for stuffed tindas

Make a thick paste by liquidising the tomatoes, onion, ginger, green chillies and dried fenugreek leaves (*kasuri methi*) with a little water and keep it aside.

Heat the oil in a saucepan and fry the paste. When it is pale brown, add the *hing*, cumin seeds, turmeric, paprika and coriander powder and garam masaala and fry for a couple of minutes. Add the salt and the water.

Add one tablespoon of cornflour, mixed to a paste with a little water. Mix well, and simmer for 10–15 minutes until it thickens. Keep it aside.

Filling and cooking the tindas

Mix together the turmeric powder, coriander powder, mango powder, chilli powder and salt and fill the *tindas* with this mixture.

Heat the oil in a wok. Add the cumin seeds and *tindas* and fry until they are golden brown. Add the water, cover and cook until fairly soft, not broken or mushy. Keep them aside.

Serving

Arrange the fried *tindas* in a serving bowl, pour the hot sauce on top (as prepared above) and leave them for 5–10 minutes.

Serve with rice or *chapaatis*.

MASAALA YAM (*MASAALA JIMIKAND*)

Ingredients

*1 small yam (peeled, cut into medium pieces – approx. 3 cm by 2 cm
and ½ cm thick – and washed)*
1 tsp salt (for boiling the yam)
1 medium onion (peeled and chopped)
1 clove garlic (peeled and chopped)
2.5 cm ginger (peeled, washed and chopped)
2 green chillies (washed and chopped)
1 tomato (washed and chopped)
1 tsp cumin seeds
1 tsp turmeric powder
1 tsp paprika powder
2 tsp coriander powder
2–3 tsp mango powder or juice of ½ lemon
1 tsp garam masaala
*1 tbs dried fenugreek leaves (*kasuri methi)
1 tsp tomato purée
½ tsp salt (according to taste)
1 tsp sugar
oil(for deep-frying the yam pieces)
3 tbs oil (for cooking)
6–7 sprigs of coriander (washed and chopped)

METHOD

Boil the yam pieces with 1 teaspoon of salt and ½ teaspoon
of turmeric powder. When soft but firm, drain and let them
dry for 5–10 minutes.

Heat the oil in a *karahi* or wok and deep-fry the boiled
pieces of yam. Keep them aside.

Heat the oil in a frying pan and fry the onion until pale

gold. Add the cumin seeds and the paprika, turmeric and coriander powder and fry for a couple of seconds. Add the chopped tomatoes, tomato purée, chopped garlic, ginger and green chillies and fry them for a couple of minutes.

Add the yam pieces and ½ teaspoon of salt and fry for 3–4 minutes. Add 2–3 cups of water and cook for 5–6 minutes. When it is semi-liquid it is ready.

Sprinkle with the garam masaala, mango powder (or lemon juice) and sugar and mix well. Decorate with chopped coriander and serve with any type of bread.

MUSHROOMS AND POTATOES (*KHUMBI AALOO*)

Ingredients

500 g (approx.) mushrooms (washed and cut into halves)
2 medium potatoes (peeled, washed and cut into medium pieces)
2.5 cm ginger (peeled, washed and chopped)
2 green chillies (washed and chopped)
1 medium onion (peeled and sliced)
2 tomatoes (cut into medium pieces)
1 tsp cumin seeds
1 tsp turmeric powder
1 tsp paprika powder
1 tsp coriander powder
½ tsp salt (according to taste)
2–3 tbs oil

METHOD

Heat the oil in a frying pan. Add the onions and fry until pale gold. Add the cumin seeds and the turmeric, paprika and coriander powder and fry for a couple of seconds. Add the tomatoes and fry them for a few minutes, then add the potatoes and fry them until golden.

Add the mushrooms, ginger, green chillies and salt. Cover and cook for a few minutes on medium heat.

The mushrooms will release their own juice on heating, which is generally sufficient for cooking.

When the potatoes and mushrooms are soft and almost dry remove the lid, and cook until completely dry.

Serve with any type of bread.

POTATOES AND CAULIFLOWER (*AALOO GOBHI*)

Ingredients

1 medium cauliflower
2–3 medium potatoes (cut into small pieces)
2.5 cm ginger (finely chopped)
3–4 green chillies (finely chopped – if you want a milder dish you can reduce the quantity of green chillies)
pinch of hing *(optional)*
2 tsp cumin seeds
¼ tsp fenugreek seeds
2 tsp coriander powder
1 tsp turmeric powder
1 tsp mango powder (optional)
1 tsp salt
3–4 tbs oil
7–8 sprigs coriander (washed and chopped)
one cup water

METHOD

Cut the cauliflower into medium florets. Cut the tender stalks and green leaves into tiny pieces. Wash well and keep aside.

Heat the oil in a frying pan. Add the *hing* and potatoes and fry them until pale gold, then add the cumin seeds, fenugreek seeds, and coriander and turmeric powder.

Fry for a couple of seconds and add the ginger, green chilli, cauliflower and salt and mix well. Cover tightly and cook on a medium heat until soft, stirring occasionally.

It is not necessary to add water. However, if the

vegetables are not tender after 10–12 minutes, add 2–3 tablespoons of water. You can add more water if required, but the vegetables should be soft, not mushy.

Add the mango powder, cover and cook for a couple of minutes. Stir well. Decorate with a sprinkle of garam masaala and chopped coriander. Serve with any sort of bread.

POTATOES AND FENUGREEK LEAVES (*AALOO METHI*)

You can buy all the following ingredients from any Asian grocer's.

Ingredients

3–4 tbs oil
2 bunches of fenugreek leaves (cleaned, chopped and washed)
2–3 medium potatoes (peeled, cut into small pieces and washed)
2–3 green chillies (washed and chopped)
pinch of hing
1 tsp cumin seeds
1 tsp turmeric powder
2 tsp coriander powder
½ tsp salt

METHOD

Clean and discard the thick stems and then chop the fenugreek leaves and wash them well so that no grit or soil remains.

Heat the oil. Add the *hing*, cumin seeds, turmeric and coriander powder and fry for a couple of seconds. Add the potatoes and fry them until pale gold, then add the fenugreek leaves, chopped green chillies and salt.

Cover and cook for approximately 8–10 minutes on medium heat until the liquid has evaporated.

Check the potatoes and cook until soft. Cook on a low heat for another 2–3 minutes until dry. Serve with any type of bread or rice.

POTATOES AND PEPPERS
(*ALOO SHIMLA MIRCH*)

Ingredients

3 peppers of any colour (washed and cut into medium pieces)
1–2 medium potatoes (peeled, washed and cut into medium pieces)
2.5 cm ginger (peeled, washed and finely chopped)
2–3 green chillies (washed and chopped – optional, or you can reduce the quantity)
1 tomato (washed and cut into medium pieces)
1 tsp cumin seeds
4–5 fennel seeds (optional, as some people do not like the fragrance)
1 tsp turmeric powder
2–3 tsp coriander powder
½ tsp salt (according to taste)
2–3 tbs cooking oil
3–4 tbs water
7 sprigs coriander (washed and chopped)

METHOD

Heat the oil in a frying pan. Add the cumin and fennel seeds and the turmeric and coriander powder. Fry for a couple of seconds, then add the ginger and tomato and fry for 2–3 minutes.

Add the potatoes and salt and fry them for 2 minutes. Add a little water.

When the potatoes are nearly soft add the chopped chillies and peppers, cover and simmer for approximately 10 minutes on a low heat. If necessary, add 1–2 tablespoons of water to soften the vegetables.

Sprinkle with chopped coriander and serve with any type of bread.

SPINACH AND POTATOES (*PAALAK AALOO*)

Ingredients

2 bunches spinach
2–3 medium potatoes (peeled, washed and cut into medium pieces)
2.5 cm ginger (peeled, washed and chopped)
pinch of hing
1 tsp cumin seeds
2 tsp coriander powder
1 tsp turmeric powder
½ tsp salt (according to taste)
2–3 tbs oil

METHOD

Clean the spinach and chop it into small pieces. Wash it 3–4 times with cold water to remove any sand or soil and keep it aside.

Heat the oil in a wok, *karahi* or frying pan. Add the *hing* and potatoes and fry for 3–4 minutes until they are pale gold.

Add the cumin seeds, coriander powder and turmeric powder and fry for a couple of seconds. Add the ginger and green chillies and fry for a couple of seconds.

Add the chopped spinach and salt. Cover and cook for a few minutes on medium heat until the potatoes are soft. The spinach will release its own juice, so do not add any water.

Remove the lid and keep cooking until it looks quite dry and well fried. If the potatoes are not soft enough add a little water, cover and continue to cook until they are. You can serve this with rice or any type of bread.

STUFFED BABY AUBERGINES (*BHARWAN CHHOTE BAINGAN*)

Ingredients

10 baby aubergines (washed and slit lengthwise in the middle, remove the stalks)
pinch of hing
1 tsp cumin seeds
1 tsp salt
1 tsp turmeric powder
¼ tsp red chilli powder
3 tsp coriander powder
2 tsp mango powder
2–3 tbs water (if necessary)

METHOD

Mix together all the ingredients except the cumin seeds and *hing*. Fill the slit baby aubergines with this mixture.

Heat the oil in a frying pan and add the *hing* and cumin seeds. When the seeds start spluttering, add the aubergines, turn down the heat, cover and simmer.

Stir them every couple of minutes until they are completely soft. Add a little water if necessary and keep cooking until dry.

Serve with rice or *chapaatis*.

STUFFED MASAALA OKRA (*BHARWAN MASAALA BHINDI*)

Ingredients

*500 g okra (*bhindi – *washed and dried with a tea towel)*
pinch of *hing*
½ tsp ajwain (smaller seeds than cumin seeds)
1 tsp cumin seeds
1 tsp turmeric powder
4 tsp coriander powder
¼ tsp chilli powder
3 tsp mango powder
1 tsp salt (according to taste)
4–5 tbs oil
5–6 sprigs of coriander (washed and chopped)
2–3 tbs water (if needed)

METHOD

Cut off the tips and tails of the okra pods (*bhindi*).

Slit the okra pods in the centre lengthwise; they should not be broken.

Mix together the salt and the turmeric, coriander, chilli and mango powder. Put this mixture (approximately ¾ tsp for a medium-sized okra pod) in the slit of each okra pod, and close it by pressing gently. If the okra pod is smaller you can reduce the quantity of the filling.

Heat the oil in a frying pan or wok and add the *hing*, ajwain and cumin seeds.

When the seeds begin spluttering, add the prepared okra pods and stir gently.

Cover and cook on medium heat.

After 3–4 minutes, stir and cover again. Turn the heat to low.

Keep stirring gently every couple of minutes until they are tender and well cooked.

If you wish, you could sprinkle with a couple of tablespoons of water to make them tender (let the water evaporate totally before removing from the heat), but generally no extra water is needed.

When they are tender and well cooked, remove the lid and stir them from time to time until they are golden brown in colour. They should be dry and soft, but not burnt or broken.

Decorate with chopped coriander and serve with any type of bread.

STUFFED PEPPERS WITH SPICY RICE (*MASAALA CHAAWAL SHIMLA MIRCH*)

Ingredients

5–6 peppers, any colour (wash, cut off the tops and save them, and remove the seeds)
¾ cup basmati rice (picked over and washed)
3 medium onions (peeled and sliced)
1 green chilli (washed and chopped)
2 tsp cumin seeds
¾ tsp salt
2 tbs oil (approx.)
1 ¾ cups water
2 tbs green coriander (chopped and washed)

METHOD

Heat the oil in a saucepan and fry the onions until golden brown. Add the cumin seeds.

After a couple of seconds add the chopped green chilli. Add the washed rice, coriander, salt and water, and cook on medium heat for approximately 10–15 minutes until the water has been absorbed and the rice is soft.

Fill the peppers with the rice mixture and cover with the saved pepper tops.

Cook in a preheated oven on a moderate heat for approximately 15–20 minutes until tender and slightly brown in colour.

Sprinkle with chopped coriander and serve with salad and bread.

You can also use other fillings, such as boiled, mashed and fried potatoes, fried onion and tomatoes and cooked dry *chana daal*.

SWEET AND SOUR PUMPKIN (*KHATTA MEETHA KADDU*)

Ingredients

1 kg (approx.) pumpkin (remove the hard skin and the seeds and cut the flesh into 2.5 cm pieces)
2.5 cm ginger (peeled, washed and chopped)
3 green chillies (washed and chopped)
pinch of hing
1 tsp cumin seeds
1 tsp fenugreek seeds
1 tsp turmeric powder
2 tsp coriander powder
3–4 tsp mango powder (if not available you can use lemon juice)
2 tsp sugar
1 tsp salt
2 tbs oil
2 cups water

METHOD

Heat the oil in a frying pan. Add the *hing*, cumin seeds, fenugreek seeds, turmeric and coriander powder and ginger. Fry them for a couple of seconds. Do not add the mango powder or lemon juice.

Add the green chillies, pumpkin pieces and salt, mix well and simmer on a low heat.

If you prefer it mushier, add 1½ cups of water. You can add more water if necessary.

When it is thoroughly soft and mushy, sprinkle with sugar and mango powder or lemon juice and cover for 5 minutes. Serve with any type of bread.

SWEET POTATO CHIPS
(*SHAKARKANDI* CHIPS)

Ingredients

2 sweet potatoes (peeled, washed and cut into chip shapes)
oil for frying
½ tsp salt
1 tsp black pepper powder
lemon juice (according to taste)

METHOD

Heat the oil in a wok or *karahi*. Fry the sweet potato chips just like ordinary chips and serve with salt and pepper.

This dish can be served as a snack or as a side dish with meals, with a dash of lemon juice or coriander chutney.

TOMATOES AND ONIONS (*TOMATO DO PIAZZA*)

Ingredients

9–10 medium tomatoes (washed and cut into quarters)
2.5 cm ginger (peeled, washed and chopped)
3 green chillies (washed and chopped – you can reduce the quantity for a milder dish)
5 medium onions (peeled and cut lengthwise)
3 tbs chopped coriander
pinch of hing
2 tsp cumin seeds
1 tsp turmeric powder
1 tsp paprika powder
2 tsp coriander powder
1 tsp salt
1 tsp sugar
4–5 tbs oil

METHOD

Heat the oil in a saucepan and add the *hing* and onions. Fry until pale gold.

Add the cumin seeds, turmeric, paprika and coriander powder. Fry for a couple of seconds.

Add the ginger and green chillies and fry for a couple of minutes. Then add the tomatoes and salt and fry for 3–4 minutes.

Simmer for 10 minutes on medium heat until the tomatoes are well cooked and the sauce has thickened. Add the sugar and simmer for a couple of minutes. Sprinkle with chopped coriander. Serve with *chapaatis, pooris, aaloo paraathas* or rice.

TURNIPS AND POTATOES
(*SHALGAM AALOO*)

Ingredients

7–8 turnips (peel, wash and cut into thin pieces, and wash and chop the green tender leaves)
2 medium potatoes (peeled, washed and cut into medium pieces)
2.5 cm ginger (peeled, washed and chopped)
2 green chillies (washed and chopped)
1 tsp cumin seeds
½ tsp fenugreek seeds
1 tsp turmeric powder
1 tsp paprika powder
2 tsp coriander powder
1 tsp salt
2 tbs oil
6–7 sprigs of coriander (washed and chopped)

METHOD

Heat the oil in a frying pan. Fry the potatoes for 5 minutes. Gradually add all the spices, the pieces of turnip, salt and chopped turnip leaves.

Cover and cook until both the vegetables are fairly soft but not mushy, adding a little water if necessary. Serve with any type of bread.

Pulses

SPLIT PULSES

WHOLE BEANS AND PULSES

Pulses

Pulses

Pulses can be used in soups and salads. They can be used in dry (*sookhi*), roasted (*bhuni*), fried (*tali*), or liquid *daal*, as a main dish with rice or any type of bread.

There are many varieties of pulses. They all have a different taste, but the cooking method is mostly similar and simple.

Whole beans, peas or lentils should be soaked overnight if possible and then cooked the next day. You can cook them the same day, but they will take at least 45 minutes to 1 hour to cook.

If you use a pressure cooker it will take much less time. Lentils should be cooked thoroughly in plenty of water until they reach the consistency of a thin sauce.

Beans, peas, lentils or split lentils should be picked over thoroughly because they can contain tiny pieces of stone and sand. Then place the lentils in a saucepan, rinse them in plenty of fresh water and discard the water. Repeat the process 2–3 times.

The word *daal* has two meanings:

1) split beans, split lentils or split peas
2) any cooked bean, pea or lentil dish

CHICKPEAS WITH VEGETABLES
(*SAFED CHANE AUR SABZI*)

Ingredients

Chickpeas

*1 cup chickpeas (soaked overnight and boiled) or 250 g canned
chickpeas (washed several times in cold water)
2.5 cm ginger (peeled, washed and chopped)
1 tsp cumin seeds
½ tsp garam masaala
1½ tsp salt
1 litre water (approx.)*

Tarka

*2 tomatoes (washed and chopped)
1 onion (peeled and chopped)
2 carrots (scraped, washed and cut into thin strips)
½ horseradish (scraped, washed and sliced into small thin strips) or
4 radishes (halved)
2 green chillies (washed and chopped)
pinch of hing
1 tsp cumin seeds
½ tsp garam masaala
3 tsp mango powder
½ tsp sugar
1 cup chopped coriander leaves
3–4 tbs oil
1 tsp cumin seeds (roasted and crushed, for sprinkling on top before
serving)*

METHOD

Chickpeas

Boil the soaked chickpeas with the salt, cumin seeds, garam masaala, and ginger in 1 litre of water. They should become mushy. Boil the canned chickpeas with spices in less water until they are mushy.

Tarka

Heat the oil in a frying pan and fry the onion with the *hing*, cumin seeds, garam masaala, green chillies and tomatoes.

When the onions are pale gold and well fried, add the sliced vegetables and fry for 5–6 minutes. Add this mixture to the chickpeas.

Add the mango powder and sugar, and simmer the chickpeas for 5–6 minutes.

Decorate the chickpeas dish with chopped coriander and roasted and crushed cumin seeds.

Serve with rice, *naan* or any type of bread. This is a north Indian speciality.

DRY URAD DAAL
(*SOOKHI URAD DAAL*)

There are two kinds of *urad daal* – with black peel or without peel (white). Whole *urad* is greyish black. You can buy this daal at any Asian grocer's. This type of dish can be made with any type of washed split *daal* (without peel).

Ingredients

1 cup washed urad daal *(without peel) soaked overnight*
2.5 cm ginger (peeled, washed and chopped)
2 green chillies (washed and chopped)
2 medium tomatoes (washed and chopped)
1 cup coriander leaves (washed and chopped)
pinch of hing
1 tsp cumin seeds
1 tsp turmeric powder
2 tsp coriander powder
1 tsp garam masaala
1 tsp salt (according to taste)
2–3 tbs oil
2–3 cups water (approx.)

METHOD

Heat the oil in a large frying pan or wok. Add the *hing*, ginger and tomatoes. Fry for a couple of minutes, then add the cumin seeds, garam masaala and the turmeric and coriander powder. Fry for another couple of seconds.

Now add the soaked and drained *urad daal*, salt and green chillies. Fry for a couple of minutes.

Add 2 cups of water and cook on medium heat until the *daal* is very soft, but not mushy.

Add a little extra water if necessary. When fully cooked all the water should have been absorbed and the *daal* should be dry (though tender).

Sprinkle with chopped coriander and serve with any type of bread.

GRAM DAAL AND CABBAGE (*BANDHGOBHI CHANA DAAL*)

Ingredients

1 small cabbage (shredded or thinly sliced and washed)
1 cup chana daal *(soaked in water overnight)*
2.5 cm ginger (peeled, washed and chopped into small pieces or grated)
1 green chilli (washed and finely chopped)
1 tomato (washed and finely cut)
5–6 sprigs green coriander (washed and chopped)
pinch of hing *(optional)*
2 tsp mustard seeds
1 tsp cumin seeds
1 tsp turmeric powder
2 tsp coriander powder
2 tsp paprika powder
½ tsp salt
3 cups water (approx. – do not add all the water at once)

METHOD

Heat the oil in a frying pan. Add the *hing*, cumin seeds, mustard seeds and the turmeric and coriander powder. Fry them for a couple of seconds. Add the ginger and tomatoes and fry them for 3–4 minutes.

Add the *daal* and the salt and fry for about 3–4 minutes. Add the green chillies and 2 cups of water, cover and simmer on a low heat until all the water has been absorbed.

Press with a spoon to see if the *daal* is tender. If not, add a little more water and then add the shredded cabbage, mix well and cover until the cabbage and *daal* are both well cooked. When it is ready it should be semi-liquid.

Serve with rice or bread.

GRAM DAAL AND COURGETTES (*TORI CHANA DAAL*)

Ingredients

1 cup gram daal *(chana daal – soaked overnight)*
1–2 courgettes (peeled, washed and cut into small pieces)
2.5 cm ginger (peeled, washed and chopped)
2 green chillies (washed and finely chopped)
½ lemon (juice)
1 medium onion (peeled and chopped)
pinch of hing
2 tsp cumin seeds
1 tsp turmeric powder
2 tsp coriander powder
1 tsp salt
8–9 sprigs coriander (washed and chopped)
3–4 tbs oil
2–3 cups (approx.) water (do not add all the water at once)

METHOD

Heat the oil, add the onions and fry until pale gold.

Add the *hing*, cumin seeds, coriander and the turmeric powder and ginger. Fry them for a couple of seconds.

Add the soaked and washed gram *daal*, and the green chillies and salt. Fry for a couple of minutes.

Add 2 cups of water and cook until the gram *daal* is completely soft. Add the courgettes. Cook them on medium heat until tender. The *daal* should not be too mushy.

Decorate with chopped coriander. Add a dash of fresh lemon juice if you wish. Serve with any type of bread.

GRAM DAAL AND GOURD
(*GHIA CHANA DAAL*)

Ingredients

1 small gourd (peeled, cut into small pieces and washed)
1 cup gram daal (chana daal – *soaked overnight)*
1 medium onion (peeled and chopped)
2.5 cm ginger (peeled, washed and chopped into small pieces)
1–2 green chillies (washed and chopped)
pinch of hing
1 tsp cumin seeds
1 tsp paprika powder
2 tsp coriander powder
1 tsp salt (according to taste)
3–4 tbs cooking oil
½ cup green coriander (washed and chopped)
3 cups (approx.) water (add gradually as needed)

METHOD

Heat the oil in a saucepan. Fry the *hing* and onion until the onion becomes golden. Add the cumin seeds, paprika, coriander powder, gram *daal* and ginger and fry for 2–3 minutes. Add the green chillies and salt and 2 cups of water, cover and cook. It should be fairly soft, but not mushy.

Add the chopped gourd and 1 more cup of water.

Cover and cook for about 10 minutes, stirring from time to time. If the gram *daal* is not soft enough, add another cup of water, or more if necessary, and simmer until soft. It should be semi-liquid. Sprinkle with chopped coriander.

This *daal* dish can be served with any type of bread or rice.

KIDNEY BEANS (*RAJMA*)

Ingredients

Kidney beans

1 cup kidney beans (soaked overnight) or 250 g can cooked kidney beans
2.5 cm ginger (peeled, washed and chopped)
1 clove garlic (peeled and chopped)
1 tsp salt
½ tsp chilli powder
1 litre water (approx.)

Tarka

1 tbs corn meal flour
1 tbs tomato purée
pinch of hing
1 tsp cumin seeds
1 tsp garam masaala
2 tsp coriander powder
1 tsp dried fenugreek leaves or 8–10 sprigs of fresh fenugreek leaves
(discard the stems, chop the leaves and wash)
3 tbs oil

METHOD

Kidney beans

Discard the soaking water and rinse the kidney beans. Boil them rapidly in 1 litre of fresh water on full heat for at least 15 minutes, then boil on medium heat for approximately 45 minutes with the salt, ginger, garlic and chilli powder until thoroughly cooked and slightly mushy.

Add extra water if necessary.

(If using canned kidney beans, boil them in ½ litre of water or more until they are mushy.)

Tarka

Heat the oil in a frying pan and add the *hing*, cumin seeds, coriander powder, garam masaala, corn meal flour (mixed with 4–5 tbs of water), tomato purée, dried fenugreek leaves and chilli powder. Fry for a couple of seconds.

Add the kidney beans and fry for approximately 1 minute. Add 1–2 cups of water and stir. Cook them for 8–10 minutes on medium heat. The consistency should be that of thick soup. Serve with rice, *chapaatis* or any type of bread.

MASAALA GRAM DAAL
(*MASAALA CHANA DAAL*)

Ingredients

1 cup gram daal *(soaked overnight or for at least a couple of hours)*
1 large tomato (washed and chopped)
2 green chillies (washed and chopped)
1 tbs tomato purée
pinch of hing
1 tsp cumin seeds
1 tsp garam masaala
1 tsp turmeric powder
1 tsp paprika powder
1 tsp coriander powder
1 tsp salt
½ bunch fresh fenugreek leaves (discard the stems, chop the leaves, wash them and keep them aside)
2–3 tbs oil
3–4 cups of water
lemon wedges

METHOD

Heat the oil in a saucepan and add the *hing*, cumin seeds, garam masaala, turmeric, coriander powder and paprika. When the seeds start spluttering add the chopped tomato and fry for 2–3 minutes.

Add the chopped fenugreek leaves, green chillies and tomato purée then add the gram *daal*, salt and water. Mix well.

Cover partly and cook for approximately 15–20 minutes until the gram *daal* is soft. Add more water if necessary, and cook until it is very soft (but not mushy) and semi-liquid.

Serve with rice or *chapaatis*, and lemon wedges (for squeezing onto the *daal* according to taste.)

MASAALA CHICKPEAS AND POTATOES
(*CHANA AALOO*)

Ingredients

2 cups chickpeas (soaked overnight, then boiled until tender)
3 medium onions (peeled and chopped)
2 medium potatoes (peeled, washed and cut into thick pieces)
2.5 cm ginger (peeled, washed and chopped)
2 green chillies (washed and thinly sliced – optional)
1 tbs dried fenugreek leaves (kasuri methi – *available in small packs at any Indian grocer's – optional*)
2 tomatoes (washed and cut into medium pieces)
1 red pepper (washed, deseeded and cut into medium pieces)
pinch of hing
2–3 tsp cumin seeds
2 tsp garam masaala
2 tsp coriander powder
1 tsp turmeric powder
1 tsp paprika powder
1 tbs tomato purée
1 tsp salt
3 tbs cooking oil
3–4 cups water (approx.)
7–8 sprigs of green coriander (washed and chopped)

METHOD

Heat the oil in a wok or frying pan. Add the *hing* and chopped onions and fry them until the onion turns pale gold. Add the potatoes and fry them until pale gold.

Add the cumin seeds, garam masaala, coriander powder, ginger and tomato purée and fry for a couple of minutes.

Add the chickpeas and fry them for about 3–4 minutes on low heat. Keep stirring every 1–2 minutes.

Add the green chillies, salt and 2 cups of water and cover.

Cook on medium heat until all the water has been absorbed.

Remove the lid to see if the potatoes are well cooked. They should be tender but not mushy. Add more water if necessary.

When ready, this dish should be semi-liquid. Sprinkle with chopped coriander and serve with any type of bread.

MASOOR DAAL

Ingredients

Daal

*1 cup red split lentils (*masoor daal *– cleaned and washed)*
1 tsp salt
2.5 cm ginger (peeled, washed and chopped)
2 green chillies (washed and chopped)
1 tsp cumin seeds
½ tsp fenugreek seeds
1 tsp turmeric powder
¼ tsp garam masaala
1 tsp coriander powder
1 litre water (approx.)

Tarka

1 onion (peeled and chopped)
1 tomato (washed and chopped)
pinch of hing
1 tsp cumin seeds
½ tsp garam masaala
2 tsp coriander powder
1 tsp paprika powder
2 tbs oil
lemon wedges
6–7 sprigs of coriander (washed and chopped)

METHOD

Daal

Put the washed *daal* and water in a saucepan and bring to the boil.

Discard any white froth that comes to the top.

Add the salt, turmeric powder, cumin seeds, coriander powder, garam masaala, chopped green chillies and ginger.

Cook on medium heat for approximately 25–30 minutes until the *daal* is quite mushy. (If you are using a pressure cooker, please check the time.)

It should have the consistency of soup, or it could be a little thicker. If required add more water.

Tarka

Heat the oil in a small frying pan and add the *hing* and onion. Fry the onion until pale gold.

Add the cumin seeds, garam masaala, coriander powder, paprika powder and chopped tomatoes and fry for a couple of minutes.

Add this fried mixture to the cooked *daal* and mix well.

Sprinkle with chopped coriander and serve with wedges of lemon.

This dish can be served with rice, *chapaatis, naan* or *paraathas*, or any other type of bread.

You can cook the following *daal* in the same way:

moong daal (split moong beans, without the peel, light yellow)

urad daal (split urad beans, without the peel, white)

toor daal (yellowish brown)

MOONG DAAL AND SPINACH (*MOONG DAAL AUR PAALAK*)

Ingredients

1 cup moong daal – *without peel (picked over, washed and soaked for at least one hour)*
2.5 cm ginger (peeled, washed and chopped)
2 green chillies (washed and chopped)
100 g (approx.) spinach (chopped and washed 3–4 times in cold water)
pinch of hing
1 tsp cumin seeds
1 tsp turmeric powder
2 tsp coriander powder
1 tsp salt
3–4 cups of water (approx.)
2–3 tbs oil

METHOD

Heat the oil in a frying pan. Add the *hing*, ginger, cumin seeds, turmeric and coriander powder and the soaked and drained *daal* and fry for 2–3 minutes.

Add the spinach, green chillies, salt and 2 cups of water, cover and cook until the moong *daal* is tender. It should be semi-liquid.

The process takes approximately 20 minutes. This dish can be semi-liquid or liquid. Add some more water for a liquid dish.

Sprinkle with chopped coriander and serve with any type of bread.

Instead of spinach you could use half a bunch of fenugreek leaves (washed and chopped).

TOOR DAAL WITH VEGETABLES (*SAMBHAR*)

Ingredients

Daal

1 cup toor daal *(cleaned and washed several times)*
1 tsp salt
1 tsp turmeric powder
1 tsp coriander powder
½ cup tamarind pulp or 1 tbs lemon juice (add when the lentils are completely cooked)
1 litre water

Tarka

1 medium onion (peeled and chopped)
1 carrot (scraped, washed and chopped into small pieces)
½ horseradish (scraped, washed and chopped – you can use a small radish if horseradish is not available)
1 small aubergine (washed and chopped)
1 tbs tomato purée
pinch of hing
2 tsp cumin seeds
1 tsp mustard seeds
¼ tsp fenugreek seeds
2 tsp coriander powder
6–7 sprigs of curry leaves (discard the stems and wash the leaves) or 6–7 sprigs of coriander leaves (washed and chopped)
3 tbs oil

METHOD

Tamarind pulp

To make tamarind pulp, soak a 3–3.5 cm block of tamarind in 2 cups of hot water for about an hour. Then mash it in the same water and filter it into a bowl. Add one cup of water to the remaining tamarind and mash and filter it. You may have to repeat the process a couple of times more. The consistency will be thicker than that of water.

If you do not want to make your own pulped tamarind you can buy it at an Asian grocer's

Daal

Put the washed *daal* and water in a saucepan and bring to the boil. If you see any white froth on the top, remove it with a ladle.

Add the salt and the turmeric and coriander powder. Cook on medium heat until the *daal* is quite mushy. (If you are using a pressure cooker, please check the time.)

Now add the tamarind pulp or lemon juice and cook for another 5 minutes. It should have the consistency of soup.

Tarka (fried spices to be added to the *daal*)

Heat the oil in a frying pan. Add the *hing* and onion and fry them until golden brown.

Add the cumin, mustard and fenugreek seeds, coriander powder and tomato purée and fry them for 1 minute. Add curry leaves if available and fry for a couple of seconds.

Add the vegetables, fry for 3–4 minutes and add to the *daal*. Sprinkle with chopped coriander and serve with *chapaatis* and rice.

WHOLE MOONG BEANS
(*SAABAT MOONG*)

Ingredients

Moong beans

1 cup whole moong beans (if soaked overnight they will not take as long to cook)
2.5 cm ginger (peeled, washed and chopped)
1 tsp cumin seeds
¼ tsp garam masaala
1 tsp turmeric powder
¼ tsp chilli powder
1 tsp coriander powder
1 tsp salt
water (at least 1 litre)

Tarka

1 medium onion (peeled and chopped – optional)
pinch of hing
1 tsp cumin seeds
1 tsp coriander powder
1 tsp paprika powder
1 tsp tomato purée
½ tsp garam masaala
7–8 sprigs of green coriander (washed and chopped)

METHOD

Moong beans

Wash the moong beans and put them in a thick-based saucepan with plenty of water. Add the salt, turmeric powder, cumin seeds, ginger, garam masaala and coriander powder.

Boil and cook on medium heat until the beans are soft (never cover fully). Cook them for approximately 45 minutes. The *daal* should be mushy and thin. If cooked in a pressure cooker the beans will take less time.

Tarka (fried spices to add to the cooked moong beans)

Heat the oil in a frying pan. Add the *hing*, chopped onion (if used,) cumin seeds, coriander and paprika powder, garam masaala and tomato purée. Fry them for a couple of minutes. Add to the moong beans and mix well. Serve with rice or any type of bread. You can cook whole masoor and whole urad in the same way.

Breads and Pancakes

METHI KE PARAATHE

DIFFERENT TYPES OF FLOUR AND *POORI*

Breads and Pancakes

Breads and Pancakes

Bread is important for life. It is a good source of protein, fibre, vitamins, iron and calcium. There are many different varieties of flour, including *chapaati* flour, plain flour, self-raising flour, wholemeal flour, semolina (fine), semolina (coarse), gram flour, corn meal flour and rice flour. I have used medium *chapaati* flour for making *chapaatis, paraathas* and *pooris* in my recipes.

CHAPAATIS (*CHAPAATI* OR *PHULKE*)

A *chapaati* is round roasted bread. It is very simple and cooks very quickly.

Ingredients
(for approx. 8–10 chapaatis*)*

3 cups medium chapaati *flour (you can buy it in an Indian grocer's)*
1 cup water (approx.)
½ cup flour (for dusting and rolling)

METHOD

Dough
Put the flour in a bowl. Add the water gradually and mix well with the flour to make a dough. If necessary, add a little more water. Knead well and keep the dough covered.

After half an hour make small balls of dough (about the size of golf balls), and using a little dry flour roll them into *chapaatis.*

The *chapaatis* should be quite thin, but you should be able to pick them up and place them on a griddle or *tava* (Indian name for a griddle).

Cooking

Cook the *chapaati* on a griddle (*tava*) on medium heat. Turn it over and, when the other side is cooked (with little brown spots), holding it with tongs take it off the griddle and cook over the flame by turning it over every two to three seconds. It will puff up and will have little brown spots. (Or cook on a griddle, pressing the edges down gently with a tea towel or kitchen paper so they puff up.) When the *chapaati* is ready, it should have little brown spots on both sides.

Spread some margarine or vegetable ghee on the puffed-up side and stack them one by one as you cook them.

CORN MEAL ROTI (*MAKKI KI ROTI*)

Ingredients

2 cups corn meal flour (fine)
2 cups wheat flour
*1 bunch fenugreek leaves (*methi*) or coriander leaves (cleaned,*
washed and chopped)
2 green chillies (finely chopped)
¼ tsp chilli powder
pinch of hing *(optional)*
1 tsp cumin seeds
½ tsp ajwain seeds (optional)
1 tsp salt
2 tsp oil
2 cups lukewarm water (add gradually)
½ cup oil (approx.) for frying the roti

METHOD

Dough

Separate and chop the fenugreek leaves. Discard the stems. Wash and chop the leaves.

Mix together the flour, chilli powder, *hing*, cumin seeds, ajwain seeds, salt, oil, fenugreek or coriander leaves and water to form a dough and knead well until smooth. Cover with a damp tea towel and keep aside for 5–10 minutes.

Rolling and frying

Put the griddle on medium heat.

Make approximately 12 balls from the dough, as for *chapaatis*.

Roll each ball into a circle about 5–6 cm in diameter.

Smear it with a few drops of oil and fold it in half.

Again smear it with a few drops of oil and fold it again. This will become a triangle shape. Roll it out thinly.

Smear a few drops of oil on the griddle. Place the *roti* on the griddle, fry for 2 minutes, then turn it over. Spread with half a teaspoon of oil and turn again. Spread some oil on this side and turn again.

Fry both sides until they are full of brown spots and look well cooked. Remove from the griddle. Keep the *rotis* in a bowl lined with kitchen paper or a tea towel.

Make all the *rotis* in the same way and stack them in the bowl. Keep them covered.

Serve them with spinach and potatoes, any vegetable masaala dish, liquid *daal*, and salad, pickle and chutney.

PARAATHAS (*PARAATHE*)

There are two types of *paraathe*, plain and savoury. When you make plain *paraathe* you make the dough exactly as for plain *chapaatis*, then add a few drops of oil and knead it. I have explained below how to cook them.

There are many varieties of savoury *paraathe*:

1) *Paraathe* stuffed with potato, onion, horseradish, potato and peas, potato and spinach, or potato and fenugreek leaves

2) Herb *paraathe* with fenugreek leaves (*methi*), coriander leaves, or mint leaves

3) Spicy *paraathe* with mixed flours such as wheat and gram flour, wheat and corn meal flour, wheat and *daal* flour, and spices.

PARAATHAS – PLAIN
(*SAADE PARAATHE*)

Ingredients

3 cups chapaati *flour*
1 tsp oil
pinch of salt
½ cup cold water (approx.)
½ cup oil (approx. – for rolling and frying)

METHOD

Dough

Put the salt, flour and 1 teaspoon of oil in a bowl and mix together well. Add the water gradually and mix to make a dough. Knead as for *chapaatis,* then leave aside for 10–15 minutes.

Frying

Heat the griddle (medium heat).

Make approximately 12 balls from the dough, as for *chapaatis.*

Take 1 ball at a time and roll it into a circle approximately 11–12 cm in diameter. Smear it with a few drops of oil and fold it in half. Smear a little more oil on this side and fold in half again. (It will change to a triangular shape.)

Roll it out again until it becomes quite thin and fairly large.

Smear a few drops of oil on the griddle. Place the *paraatha* on the griddle and fry for 2 minutes. Spread 1–2 teaspoons of oil on top, then turn it over.

Fry both sides until full of brown spots, then remove

from the griddle. Keep it in a dish or on a plate lined with kitchen paper or a tea towel.

Make all the *paraathe* in the same way and stack them in the dish or on the plate. Keep them covered.

Serve them with any vegetable dish and chutney.

PARAATHAS WITH FENUGREEK LEAVES
(*METHI PARAATHE*)

Ingredients

3 cups wheat flour
1 cup gram flour
*1 bunch green fenugreek leaves (*methi ki patti*)*
pinch of hing *(optional)*
2 tsp cumin seeds
½ tsp chilli powder
2 tsp coriander powder
1 tsp salt
1 tsp oil
2 cup lukewarm water
oil for rolling and frying paraathe *(approx. ½ cup, or more if needed)*

METHOD

Dough

Separate the fenugreek leaves, throw away the stems and chop the leaves into small pieces. Wash them thoroughly in a sieve or colander and keep them aside.

Mix together the flour, *hing*, cumin seeds, chilli and coriander powder, 1 teaspoon oil, salt, fenugreek leaves and water (add gradually) to make a dough, and knead well until smooth.

Make in the same way as plain *paraathe*.

(Instead of fenugreek leaves you could use coriander leaves or mint leaves.)

Note: If you do not wish to use gram flour, you can just use wheat flour (4 cups).

Rolling and Frying

Put the griddle on medium heat.

Make 12 balls from the dough, as for *chapaatis*.

Take 1 ball and roll it into a circle about 10–12 cm in diameter, smear it with a few drops of oil and fold it in half. Again, smear it with a few drops of oil and fold it into a triangle shape. Roll it out thinly.

Smear a few drops of oil on the griddle.

Spread the *paraatha* pastry on the griddle, cook for a minute or two, then turn it over, spread with ½ teaspoon of oil and turn it over again. Again, spread the oil on this side and turn it over again.

Fry both sides until they are full of brown spots. Remove the *paraatha* from the griddle.

Keep it in a bowl lined with kitchen paper or a tea towel.

Make all the *paraathe* in the same way and stack them in the bowl. You can serve them with potatoes and peas (*aaloo matar*) or any other masaala vegetable dish and chutney.

PARAATHAS STUFFED WITH POTATO
(*AALOO PARAATHE*)

Ingredients

Filling

4–5 medium potatoes (washed, boiled, peeled and mashed)
2.5 cm ginger (peeled, washed and chopped)
2 tsp cumin seeds
1 tsp chilli powder
¼ tsp garam masaala
1 tsp paprika powder
½ tsp salt
1 tsp oil

Dough

4 cups medium chapaati *flour*
1 cup flour (for dusting and rolling)
2 cup water (lukewarm)
1 tsp salt
8–10 sprigs of coriander leaves (cleaned, washed and chopped)
1 tsp cumin seeds
1 tsp oil
½ cup oil (approx. – for rolling and frying)

METHOD

Filling

Mix the ginger, chilli powder, garam masaala, cumin seeds, paprika powder, salt and 1 teaspoon oil into the potatoes and mash them well. Keep aside. (If you wish to add onion, peel and finely chop 1 onion and mix with the filling.)

Dough

Mix the flour, salt, cumin seeds, chopped coriander leaves and 1 teaspoon oil together to make a dough and knead until smooth.

Rolling and Frying

Make small balls from the dough (approx.12–14). Take 1 at a time and roll it into a circle approximately 8–10 cm in diameter. Sprinkle a few drops of oil on the surface and spread it over the circle.

Put 1 dessert spoon of filling in each circle. Cover the filling by pleating the pastry all round and bringing the edges together, making it as flat as possible. Roll out into a circle again, 15–18 cm in diameter, starting at the edges and using a little flour.

Heat a griddle or *tava*, spread with a teaspoon of oil, and put the rolled *paraatha* on the medium hot griddle.

First cook on one side and sprinkle with 1–2 teaspoons of oil. Turn it over carefully and spread with a little oil again.

When both sides are well cooked and have little brown spots, place the *paraatha* in a dish lined with kitchen paper or a tea towel and cover tightly.

Roll and cook all the *paraathe* in the same way (approximately 12–14 *paraathe*).

Serve with vegan margarine, tomato chutney or pickle, and salad.

They are delicious. You can make different fillings with mashed potatoes such as *aaloo matar* (potatoes and peas), *aaloo methi* (potatoes and fenugreek leaves) and *aaloo paalak* (potatoes and spinach).

PARAATHAS STUFFED WITH HORSERADISH (*MOOLI PARAATHE*)

Mooli paraathe (Indian fried bread) are very tasty and they are a delicacy. They need careful rolling otherwise they will stick to the rolling pin.

Ingredients

Filling

1 large horseradish (scraped, washed and grated)
2.5 cm ginger (peeled, washed and chopped)
2 green chillies (washed and finely chopped) or ½ tsp chilli powder
3 tsp coriander powder
½ tsp garam masaala
1 tsp cumin seeds
1tsp salt
½ tsp oil

Dough

5 cups flour
8–10 sprigs of coriander leaves (washed and chopped.)
1 tsp salt
1 tsp cumin seeds
1 tsp ajwain seeds (if available – you can buy them from an Indian grocer's)
1 cup flour (for dusting)
2 cup water (lukewarm)
1 tsp oil

METHOD

Filling

Remove both ends of the horseradish, then scrub, wash and grate. Add the salt, mix well, cover and keep aside for 15–20 minutes.

Squeeze most of the water out of the grated radish with your hands.

Add the green chillies or chilli powder, cumin seeds, garam masaala, coriander powder to the grated radish, mix well and keep aside.

Dough

Mix the flour, salt, coriander leaves, cumin seeds, ajwain seeds and 1 teaspoon oil together to make a smooth dough.

Rolling and Frying

Make small balls, as for *chapaatis* (approximately 14).

Take 1 ball at a time and roll it into a circle of 8–9 cm diameter. Sprinkle with a few drops of oil and spread the oil over the surface.

Put 1 dessert spoon of filling in each circle, pleat all the sides and join them together, then roll them one by one, using a little flour, until 12–14 cm in diameter.

Heat a griddle or *tava*, spread with a little oil, and cook 1 *paraatha* at a time.

First cook on one side, then turn it, spread some oil on the surface with a spoon, and then repeat the same process on the other side.

When both sides are well cooked and have little brown spots, place the *paraatha* in a dish lined with kitchen paper or tea towel and cover tightly.

Cook all the *paraathe* in the same way (approximately 12–14 *paraathe*). Serve with vegan margarine, pickle, *daal* or any masaala vegetable dish.

PARAATHAS WITH ONIONS OR LEEKS
(*PIAZ WAALE PARAATHE*)

Ingredients

2 large onions (peeled and finely chopped) or 4 leeks (washed, dried and finely chopped)
4 cups medium chapaati *flour*
1 tsp cumin seeds
1 tsp salt
2 tsp oil
8–9 sprigs coriander (washed and chopped)
1½ cups lukewarm water (approx.)
½ cup flour (approx. – for dusting)
oil (for rolling and frying)

METHOD

Dough

Place the 4 cups of flour, cumin seeds, salt, chopped coriander and onions or leeks in a bowl and mix well together. Add the water gradually to form a soft dough, then knead it well.

Add a few drops of oil and knead the dough until smooth. Keep it aside for 15–20 minutes then make the *paraathe* – approximately 10–12.

Rolling and frying

First make a small ball of dough (as for *chapaatis*). Roll it into a circle approximately 6–7 cm in diameter. Spread a little oil on it with a spoon and fold in half.

Again spread a little oil, fold it into a triangle, and roll out until 10–12 cm long and approximately ¼ cm thick.

Heat a griddle to medium temperature. Smear a little oil on the griddle and spread the rolled *paraatha* pastry over it.

When it is partly cooked, turn it over and spread approximately one teaspoon of oil over it, then turn it over again. Spread a teaspoon of oil on this side as well and turn it and cook both sides until they are full of golden brown spots.

Keep it aside in a bowl lined with kitchen paper and cover it tightly to keep it soft.

Cook all the *paraathe* in the same way and stack them in a bowl. Serve them with *aaloo matar* or any vegetable dish, coriander and mint chutney and salad.

If you do not wish to cook a vegetable dish you can eat the *paraathe* with any pickle or mango chutney, or just on their own.

POORIS

A *poori* is an Indian deep-fried bread. It cooks very quickly. *Pooris* are good for quick dinners, Sunday brunch, or parties. *Pooris* can be made plain, savoury or stuffed.

PLAIN POORIS (*SAADI POORI*)

Ingredients

3 cups chapaati *flour*
1 cup plain white flour
1 tbs oil
¼ tsp salt
1½ cups lukewarm water (approx.)
oil for deep frying

METHOD

Dough

Mix together the flour, salt and 1 tablespoon of oil in a large steel or glass bowl. (I mostly use a shallow, wide metallic bowl called a *paraat*. It is easier to knead the dough in the *paraat*.)

Add the water gradually to form a dough. (Do not add all the water at once, because you may not need all of it.)

Knead it until smooth. It should be firmer than the *chapaati* or *paraatha* dough, because dusting flour is not used for rolling the *pooris*. (It makes the oil cloudy when you fry the *pooris*, so try to avoid it.)

You can use a drop of oil on your pastry board.

Rolling

Make small balls from the dough. The above quantities will make approximately 16–18 *pooris*.

Using a drop of oil on your pastry board, roll each ball into a circle approximately 6–7 cm in diameter. Roll out approximately 7–8 *pooris* at a time ready for frying. Cover them with a slightly damp tea towel and keep aside.

Frying

Heat the oil in a wok or *karahi* for deep-frying and fry the *pooris* one or two at a time.

They will puff up. Turn over and fry gently for 1 minute, and remove from the wok when they are pale gold in colour. (Ensure you do not splash drops of oil on yourself.)

You can serve them hot, or if you want to keep them for some time, wrap them in tinfoil. (This will keep them soft.)

They can be served with any liquid masaala vegetable dish, dry vegetable dish or *daal*.

(You have to take extra care when cooking with boiling oil – make sure it does not become too hot. Regulate the heat by reducing and increasing the setting.)

POORIS STUFFED WITH DAAL
(*DAAL POORI*)

Ingredients

Filling

1 cup urad daal *(soaked overnight then crushed or lightly ground)*
2.5 cm ginger (peeled, washed and grated)
½ tsp hing *(optional)*
½ tsp salt
2 tsp cumin seeds
7–8 fennel seeds (roasted and crushed)
2 tsp coriander powder
½ tsp red chilli powder
1 tbs oil

Dough

3 cups medium chapaati *flour*
2 cups plain white flour
2 tbs oil
1 tsp salt
2 cups lukewarm water (approx.)
oil for frying

METHOD

Filling

Heat the oil in a frying pan. Add the *hing*, cumin seeds and chilli and coriander powder. Fry for a couple of seconds. Add the ginger, *daal* and salt and fry for 7–8 minutes until pale brown. Keep stirring. When well fried, keep the filling on one side.

Dough

Place the flour in a mixing bowl. Add the salt and oil.

Add the warm water gradually to form a large ball of dough, and knead until smooth.

Rolling

Make approximately 14–15 smaller balls out of the large ball.

Take one at a time and roll into a circle approximately 7–8 cm in diameter.

Put 1 teaspoon of filling in the centre, bring all the edges together and seal them (in a round shape) with a drop of water.

Roll until approximately13–15 cm in diameter. Make all the *pooris* in the same way and keep them aside and cover them.

Frying

Heat the oil and fry the *pooris* on a medium heat (2–3 at a time) until pale gold.

You can serve them with *koftas* in masaala sauce, potatoes and peas or any other liquid masaala vegetable dish, plus chutney, mango pickle and salad.

SAVOURY GRAM FLOUR PANCAKES (*BESAN CHEELE*)

Ingredients

3 cups besan *(gram flour)*
1 small onion (peeled and finely chopped)
2–3 cups of water (approx.)
pinch of hing
2 tsp cumin seeds
1 tsp salt
2–3 tsp coriander powder
1 tsp chilli powder (you can reduce the quantity if you wish)
1 cup green coriander (chopped and washed)
1 cup oil for frying (approx.)

METHOD

Batter

Make the batter in a large bowl with the gram flour, *hing,* salt, cumin seeds, coriander and chilli powder and water. Add the water gradually and keep stirring until the batter reaches a thick pouring consistency. (You may not need all the water or you may need more, depending upon the thickness of the batter.)

Add the chopped onions and green coriander. Keep the batter aside for at least 10–15 minutes.

Frying

Heat a griddle and grease with 1 teaspoon of oil. Spread one ladle of batter over it (it should look like a very thin *chapaati* – a circle 8–9 cm in diameter).

Smear the sides of the pancake (*cheela*) with the oil. After

1 minute turn it over with a spatula. Fry both sides until brown and well cooked.

Keep the cooked pancakes in a bowl lined with kitchen paper. Serve them hot with sweet mango chutney, mango pickle or coriander and mint chutney.

SEMOLINA PANCAKES (*SUJI DOSA*)

A *dosa* is a kind of a pancake. It is a south Indian dish.

Ingredients

3 cups semolina
2 sprigs green curry leaves (discard the stems and wash the leaves)
3–4 cups water (approx.)
2 tsp mustard seeds
pinch of hing
1 tsp salt
½ tsp sugar
1 onion (peeled and finely chopped)
oil for frying

METHOD

Batter

Make the batter in a large bowl with the semolina, sugar, salt and water. Add the water gradually until the batter reaches a pouring consistency.

Leave the batter in a warm place for 5–6 hours.

Add the onion and keep the batter aside.

Heat 1 tablespoon of oil in a small frying pan. Add the *hing* and mustard seeds. When they start to splutter, add the curry leaves.

Let them cool for a few seconds and then mix them into the batter.

Frying

Heat a griddle or *tava*. Grease with a little oil and spread with 1½ ladles of batter to form a round shape, the size of a *chapaati*. Pour 1 teaspoon of oil on the edges of the *dosa*.

When it is cooked underneath, turn it over carefully. Spread a little oil on this side, and cook until golden brown.

Make all the semolina pancakes in the same way and serve hot with sweet and sour toor *daal* (*sambhar*) and coconut chutney.

TANDOORI BAKED BREAD (*NAAN*)

Naan is a very popular type of bread. It is useful for parties because you can cook it in advance and keep it for a few days, wrapped in a tin foil or a polythene food bag. Spread some vegan margarine on each *naan* and serve hot.

I prefer homemade *naan* bread because you can choose the size, softness and ingredients.

Ingredients

4 cups self-raising flour
1 tsp bicarbonate soda
2 cup (approx.) soya milk (lukewarm)
2 tbs margarine
1 tsp sugar
½ tsp salt
*2 tsp onion seeds (*kalonji*)*

METHOD

Dough

Mix the flour with all other ingredients adding the soya milk gradually to form a dough. Knead until soft. Keep it for 7–8 hours or overnight in a warm place. Cover with a polythene bag.

The dough will gradually rise and almost double in size. It will now be ready to cook.

Rolling and shaping

Make the dough into balls (the size of a golf balls). Smear a few drops of oil in your palm, rub it over dough ball, and then roll it into a circle approximately 8–9 cm in diameter.

(If you find it difficult to roll, you can use dry flour.)

Next, hold the edges with your right hand and pull it into an oblong or *naan* shape, approximately13–15 cm in length.

Figure 2:

Naan

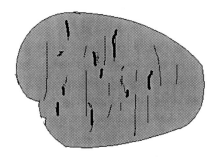

Cooking

Use a griddle for cooking and keep it on medium heat.

Place 1 *naan* on the griddle and cook 1 side until lightly brown. Now brown the other side under a hot grill. (If you find it difficult, brown the other side on the griddle as well.)

It will puff up. When it is brown, remove from the grill or griddle. Spread with margarine on the puffed side and keep it aside, covered with a tea towel.

Cook all the *naans* in the same way and wrap them in foil to keep them warm and soft.

If necessary, they can be reheated in the microwave for a few seconds after sprinkling with a few drops of water, or on the griddle for a minute or two. They can also be sprinkled with a little water, wrapped in foil and put in a hot oven for 5–6 minutes.

Serve them with *daal, koftas* in masaala sauce, or any semi-liquid masaala dish, plus salad, pickle and chutney.

Rice Dishes

DIFFERENT TYPES OF RICE

BROWN RICE, BASMATI RICE AND EASY-COOK RICE

Rice Dishes

Rice Dishes

Rice is a good source of carbohydrate. There are many varieties of rice. The most popular and widely used are: easy cook, long grain, basmati, risotto and brown rice. Brown rice takes approximately twice the amount of water and time to cook as white rice.

In this book I am only using basmati rice, unless otherwise stated. Cooking rice well takes some practice. You have to get used to the quality of the rice. It is said that older rice is best. The reason is that new rice absorbs less water, while older rice absorbs more water. You should always add a few drops of oil while cooking rice because it keeps the rice fluffy and prevents the grains from sticking together.

The following are different varieties of savoury rice:

- When you mix lentils with rice it is called *khichri*. *Khichri* can be dry or semi – liquid.
- Pilau is fried and cooked rice with different vegetables or pulses. (Only one or two in each dish.)
- For cooking all rice dishes use a large and deep saucepan.

PLAIN RICE (*SAADE CHAAWAL*)

Plain rice can be cooked in two ways:

- Boiling in a large amount of water
- Cooking by measured water

PLAIN RICE (BOILED)

Ingredients

1 cup rice (picked over and washed several times)
1 tsp oil
plenty of water (at least 6 times the volume of rice using a cup as a measure for both)

METHOD

Boil the water in a large saucepan. Add a few drops of oil. When it starts boiling, add the washed rice.

Boil briskly for about 5 minutes, then take out a few grains of rice and press them between your finger and thumb to check that they are soft. The rice is ready if soft.

Drain the water and put the rice on a very low heat for a few minutes to dry it. Add 1 teaspoon of oil and mix it in with a fork.

This method is good if you are not sure about the exact amount of water needed to cook the rice.

PLAIN RICE (MEASURED WATER)

Ingredients

1 cup rice (picked over and washed 3–4 times)
1 tsp oil
2 cups water

METHOD

Put the rice and water in a medium-sized saucepan and place on medium heat. Add the oil.

When the water starts boiling reduce the heat, cover and simmer for 5 minutes.

Check the rice. Turn the heat to very low and cook until the grains become soft, but not mushy, and all the water has been absorbed.

Serve with *daal* or any liquid vegetable dish, roasted aubergine, and coriander and mint chutney, or serve with *daal,* mango pickle and *paapad* (pappadom).

GRAM DAAL KHICHRI, DRY (*CHANA DAAL KI SUKHI KHICHRI*)

Ingredients

1 cup gram daal *(chana daal – picked over, washed and soaked for at least 4 hours)*
1 cup rice (picked over and washed)
1–2 green chillies (washed and very finely chopped – optional)
1 large onion (peeled and chopped)
2 tsp cumin seeds
1 tsp paprika powder
1 tsp turmeric powder
1 tsp salt (according to taste)
4–5 tbs oil
4 cups (approx.) water (for gram daal*)*
2 ½ cups water (for khichri*)*
8–10 sprigs of coriander (washed and chopped)

METHOD

Heat the oil in a saucepan. Fry the onion until golden brown, then add the soaked, washed and drained gram *daal*, cumin seeds, paprika and turmeric powder, salt and chopped green chillies.

Fry for 5 minutes, then add 3 cups of water. Use more water if necessary.

Bring to the boil, then cook on medium heat until soft, but not mushy.

When all the water has been absorbed, add the washed rice, chopped coriander and 2½ cups of water.

When it starts boiling, turn the heat down to low, cover and cook for approximately 10 minutes. Make sure it is well cooked and nearly dry. Serve with tomato chutney, sweet mango chutney, mango pickle and *paapad*.

MOONG DAAL KHICHRI
SEMI LIQUID
(*MOONG DAAL KI GEELI KHICHRI*)

Moong daal khichri is a special preparation of mixed rice and lentils. It is a very tasty and easily digestible food. It is considered good during convalescence.

Ingredients

Khichri

1 cup rice (picked over and washed)
½ cup moong daal, *yellow* (dhuli moong daal – *picked over and washed)*
7–8 sprigs green coriander (chopped and washed)
2.5 cm ginger (washed and chopped)
1 tsp cumin seeds
1½ tsp salt
1 tsp turmeric powder
¼ tsp garam masaala
7–8 cups of water (approx.)

Tarka

½ tsp hing
2 tsp cumin seeds
¼ tsp garam masaala
3 tbs vegetable ghee or oil

METHOD

Khichri

Wash the rice in a large saucepan and drain. Add the washed

moong *daal,* ginger, salt, turmeric powder, garam masaala, cumin seeds and water.

Boil for 5–7 minutes, turn the heat down to low and cook until the rice and *daal* are soft. Both should be mixed together well and should be semi-liquid. Add more water if necessary.

Tarka

Heat the oil in a frying pan and fry the cumin seeds, *hing* and garam masaala for a few seconds, add them to the *khichri* and mix well.

Sprinkle with chopped green coriander and serve hot with pickle, *paapad* and chutney on a plate or in a bowl.

BLACK-EYED BEANS PILAU (*RONGI KE CHAAWAL*)

Black-eyed beans need to be cooked carefully to prevent them becoming mushy.

Ingredients

¾ cup black-eyed beans (washed and boiled)
1 cup rice (cleaned and washed)
2.5 cm ginger (peeled and chopped)
2 green chillies (very finely chopped – optional)
1 large onion (peeled and chopped)
1 tsp cumin seeds
1 tsp paprika powder
1 tsp turmeric powder (optional)
1½ tsp salt (according to taste)
4 tbs oil
2¼ cups of water
7–8 sprigs of green coriander (washed and chopped)

METHOD

Heat the oil in a saucepan. Fry the onion until golden brown, then add the cumin seeds, turmeric and paprika powder and black-eyed beans (soaked, washed and boiled, tender but not mushy).

Fry for 2–3 minutes, then add the washed rice, salt, chopped coriander and water.

When the water starts boiling, turn the heat down to medium. Cover and cook for approximately 10–12 minutes. Ensure the rice is well cooked and all the water has been absorbed.

Serve with tomato chutney, mango pickle and pappadoms (*paapad*).

CAULIFLOWER PILAU
(*GOBHI KE CHAAWAL*)

This is a very tasty and attractive-looking pilau. The cauliflower needs to be fried carefully so the florets do not break.

Ingredients

1½ cups rice (picked over and washed)
1 medium cauliflower (cut florets lengthwise approx. 3 cm. Slice them in half and wash)
2.5 cm ginger (peeled, washed, and chopped)
1 large onion (peeled and sliced lengthwise)
2 tsp cumin seeds
1 tsp paprika powder
1 tsp turmeric powder (optional)
½ tsp chilli powder
1 tsp salt (according to taste)
3 tbs oil
3 cups water
7–8 sprigs of coriander (washed and chopped)

METHOD

Heat the oil in a saucepan. Fry the onion until pale gold. Add the cumin seeds, paprika, turmeric and chilli powder, cauliflower and ginger and fry them for approximately two minutes, stirring continuously.

Now add the rice, salt, chopped coriander and water. Cover and simmer for 10–12 minutes. When the rice and cauliflower are soft and nearly dry, the pilau is ready.

ONION PILAU
(*PIAZ WAALE CHAAWAL*)

Ingredients

1 cup basmati rice (for any other kind of rice, read the instructions on the packet to adjust the amount of water)
2 large onions (peeled and sliced lengthwise)
9–10 sprigs of coriander (washed and chopped)
2 tsp cumin seeds
1 tsp salt
1 tsp paprika powder
½ tsp garam masaala
1 tsp turmeric powder (optional)
4–5 tbs oil
2½ cups water (for brown rice you need 6 cups approx.)

METHOD

Heat the oil in a saucepan and fry the onion until golden brown.

Add the cumin seeds, garam masaala, turmeric powder and paprika powder and fry for a couple of seconds.

Add the rice, chopped coriander, water and salt. Cook on a medium heat. When it starts to boil, reduce to a low heat.

When the rice has absorbed all the water, the grains should be soft (check them by pressing with thumb and fingers).

Serve with *koftas* in masaala sauce or any liquid masaala vegetable dish, and tomato chutney, green chutney or any other pickle.

Instead of onion, you could use leeks or spring onions.

POTATO PILAU
(*AALOO WAALE CHAAWAL*)

Ingredients

2–3 medium potatoes (washed and cut into small pieces)
1 onion (peeled and chopped)
1 tomato (washed and cut into small pieces)
2 green chillies (washed and chopped)
1½ cups rice (picked over and washed)
2 tsp cumin seeds
1 tsp mustard seeds
½ tsp garam masaala
1 tsp turmeric powder
1 tsp salt (according to taste)
3 cups water
7–8 sprigs of coriander leaves (washed and chopped)

METHOD

Heat the oil in a saucepan. Fry the onion, tomato and ginger. Add the cumin seeds, mustard seeds, *garam masaala* and turmeric powder. Fry them for a couple of seconds, then add the potatoes and green chillies.

Fry until the potatoes become pale gold then add the rice, salt and coriander leaves. Add the water. When it starts boiling, turn down the heat and simmer for 5 minutes.

When the rice is soft and almost dry, the pilau is ready.

Serve with fried *paapad*, plum chutney, sweet mango chutney, tomato chutney or hot coriander and mint chutney.

Pickles and Chutneys

INGREDIENTS FOR PICKLES AND CHUTNEYS: APPLE,
TAMARIND, SULTANAS, GINGER AND GARLIC

GREEN CORIANDER, RED AND GREEN CHILLIES AND LEMONS

Pickles and Chutneys

Pickles and Chutneys

We preserve fresh vegetables and fruits by pickling or by making chutneys. Most of the vegetables and fruits retain their vitamins and minerals, though they become very salty. Oil, salt and lemon all preserve vegetables. Sugar can preserve fruits. Pickles and chutneys are appetising and tasty.

APPLE AND PLUM CHUTNEY (*SEB AUR ALOOCHA CHUTNI*)

Ingredients

4 Granny Smith apples or any sweet and sour apples (peeled and cut into small pieces)
4 plums (washed and chopped into small pieces)
4–5 green chillies (washed and chopped)
2.5 cm ginger (peeled, washed and chopped)
1 tbs raisins
1 tbs oil
pinch of hing
1 tsp cumin seeds
1 tsp fenugreek seeds
½ tsp garam masaala
½ tsp salt
3 tsp sugar

METHOD

Heat the oil in a saucepan. Add the cumin and fenugreek seeds. When they start to splutter, add the garam masaala, salt, ginger, green chillies, chopped apples and plums.

When everything is soft (approximately 5–7 minutes), add the sugar and raisins and simmer for 2–3 minutes until fairly thick.

Serve hot or cold with any type of *paraathas*, savoury pancakes or rice.

COCONUT CHUTNEY
(*NAARIYAL CHUTNI*)

Ingredients

1 cup grated coconut (dry or fresh naariyal*)*
¾ cup chana daal
3–4 green chillies (washed and chopped)
2 lemons (juice)
pinch of hing
1 tsp mustard seeds
1 tsp salt
8–10 curry leaves (to enhance the taste and aroma)
2 tsp oil
2½ cups water (approx.)

METHOD

Heat a griddle or frying pan and roast the chana *daal* until it is lightly brown.

Put the grated coconut, chana *daal*, green chillies, lemon juice, and salt in a liquidiser and add the water gradually. Make into a thick paste and pour into a bowl.

Heat the oil in a small frying pan. Add the *hing*, mustard seeds and curry leaves.

When the seeds start spluttering, remove them from the heat and add them to the chutney. Leave the chutney to cool.

Serve with semolina pancakes (*dosa* – south Indian dish.) This chutney can be eaten with any type of food (avoid eating the curry leaves). It is delicious.

GREEN CORIANDER AND MINT CHUTNEY
(HARAA DHANIYA AUR PUDINA CHUTNI)

In Indian cookery, herb chutneys, herb decoration and cooking with herbs are a speciality. Green coriander and mint are very tasty herbs, though both of them are a little pungent. Green coriander is used liberally in liquid vegetable dishes, salads, rice, pilau and chutneys. It is considered good for the stomach and heart. Mint is well known for its coolness and digestive qualities.

Ingredients

1 bunch coriander (washed and chopped)
½ bunch mint (stems removed, leaves washed and chopped)
12 green chillies (washed, chopped and stems removed– these are hot, so you may use fewer chillies according to your taste if you want a milder chutney)
5–6 cm ginger (peeled washed and cut in small pieces)
2 pods garlic (peeled and chopped – optional)
2 lemons (juice)
2 tsp cumin seeds
pinch of hing
1 tsp salt (according to taste)
4–5 tbs (approx.) water (for liquidising)

METHOD

Liquidise all the ingredients except the cumin seeds and *hing*.

Roast the cumin seeds and *hing* for a couple of seconds and grind. Add to the chutney and mix well. The chutney should have the consistency of a thick sauce.

Serve the chutney with any type of food. It can be stored in a fridge for up to 2 weeks.

STAR FRUIT AND GREEN CHILLI CHUTNEY
(*KAMRAKH AUR HARI MIRCH CHUTNI*)

You will find star fruit in the large stores or an Asian grocery shop. This fruit is rich in vitamin C and very tasty if you make it spicy.

Ingredients

3 star fruits (washed, dried and cut into small pieces – triangles or rounds)
4 green chillies (washed and chopped)
4–5 sprigs of green coriander (washed and chopped)
2.5 cm ginger (peeled, washed and chopped)
pinch of hing
1 tsp cumin seeds
½ tsp fenugreek seeds
½ tsp fenugreek seeds (roasted and ground – for sprinkling afterwards)
½ tsp salt
3 tsp sugar
1 tbs oil
1 cup water

(Some people do not like the bitter taste of fenugreek seeds, but these seeds have a wonderful aroma if roasted until pale brown, ground and sprinkled. In this recipe you can sprinkle ½ teaspoon on the chutney when it is ready.)

METHOD

Heat the oil in a saucepan. Add the *hing*, cumin seeds and fenugreek seeds. When they start to splutter, add the ginger, green chillies, star fruit, water and salt.

Cook for 5 minutes on a medium heat. If still not tender enough, you can add some extra water.

Now add the sugar and cook for another 2–3 minutes.

Sprinkle with chopped coriander and roasted fenugreek seeds and serve as an accompaniment with rice or *chapaatis*.

SWEET AND SOUR TAMARIND CHUTNEY
(*KHATTI MEETHI IMLI KI SAUNTH*)

Ingredients

*50 g tamarind (washed and soaked overnight or soaked in hot water
for a few hours – approx. 2 cups)*
6–7 prunes (soaked overnight and thinly sliced)
1 tsp salt (according to taste)
50 g sugar
¼ tsp hing
2 tsp cumin seeds

METHOD

Tamarind pulp

Wash your hands and dry them well. Mash the soaked tamarind with your hand. Add ½ cup of water and discard the tamarind (*imli*) seeds and fibre.

Chutney

Place the tamarind pulp in a saucepan and add the salt, sugar, and prunes. Bring to the boil, then simmer for 5 minutes. When it thickens (thick sauce consistency), remove from the heat.

Roast the cumin seeds and *hing* on a griddle. As soon as the seeds start spluttering, remove from the heat. Crush with a rolling pin and add to the chutney. Mix well and cool.

This chutney (*saunth*) is a good accompaniment with snacks such as *pakoras,* samosas or *bhelpoori chaat*.

SWEET MANGO CHUTNEY (*AAM KI MEETHI ACHAARI*)

Ingredients

500 g hard, green, raw mangoes (peel and grate, and remove the stones)
700 g sugar
3 tsp salt
1 tsp hing
2 tsp cumin seeds
1 tbs black pepper (roughly ground)
1 stick cinnamon (powdered)
¼ tsp red chilli powder
2 tsp cardamom seeds, large, black (powdered)

METHOD

Mix the grated mango with the salt and *hing* in a large glass bowl (2 kilo) and leave it overnight.

On the second day, place the grated mangoes in a thick-based steel saucepan, add the sugar, cumin seeds, ground black pepper, cinnamon and black cardamom powder and place on a medium heat.

Simmer and stir until it becomes dry and reaches a thick consistency with a transparent look.

Leave it to cool. When it is quite cold, transfer to a jar. This chutney (*achaari*) stays fresh for a long time (approximately 2–3 months).

Sweet mango chutney is a favourite accompaniment with many savoury snacks and meals.

TOMATO AND ONION CHUTNEY (*TAMAATAR AUR PIAZ KI CHUTNI*)

Ingredients

980 g tomatoes (washed and cut into medium pieces)
2 onions (peeled and finely cut)
2 cloves garlic (peeled, washed and chopped)
1–2 green chillies (washed and chopped) – optional
1–2 tbs oil (olive oil or vegetable oil)
1 tsp sugar
½ tsp salt
1 tsp mixed herbs (oregano, marjoram, and basil)
1 cup water
1 tsp cornflour (mixed with a little cold water before adding)

METHOD

Liquidise the tomatoes, garlic, ginger and chillies.

Fry the onions in a saucepan and add the liquidised mixture of tomatoes, ginger and chillies. Add the cornflour, salt and sugar.

Simmer for approximately 8–10 minutes, or until it becomes a thick sauce consistency.

Serve this chutney with rice, pasta or savoury snacks.

TOMATO CHUTNEY
(*TAMAATAR KI CHUTNI*)

Ingredients

500 g tomatoes
2.5 cm ginger (chopped)
3–4 green chillies (chopped)
½ tsp salt (according to taste)
pinch of hing
1 tsp cumin seeds
½ tsp fenugreek seeds
2 tsp coriander powder
1 tsp sugar
3–4 sprigs of coriander (washed and chopped)

METHOD

Boil some water in a saucepan, then add the tomatoes and let them boil for 2–3 minutes.

When their skins split, remove from the heat, let them cool, then peel (discard the skin) and cut into small pieces.

Heat the oil in a saucepan. Add the spices, then the ginger, green chillies, salt and tomatoes and fry for a couple of minutes. Cover and cook for 5 minutes on medium heat.

Add the sugar and cook for another 2–3 minutes. Mash well, and sprinkle with chopped coriander.

Serve with *aaloo paraathas,* savoury rice, or with snacks.

GARLIC, GREEN CHILLI AND GINGER PICKLE IN LEMON (*LAHSUN, HARI MIRCH, ADRAK AUR NIMBU KA ACHAAR*)

This is very refreshing and tasty, and can be served with any type of food. It is considered good for digestion.

Ingredients

2 whole garlic bulbs (peel the cloves and cut each one of them in half)
5 green chillies (washed and cut into 1 cm pieces)
7–8 cm ginger (peeled, washed and cut into small pieces)
juice of 2 lemons
2 tsp salt

METHOD

Mix together all the ingredients and put them in a glass jar.

Shake twice daily. The pickle will be ready in 2–3 days. It can be kept in the fridge for about 2 weeks, and is a good accompaniment with any kind of food.

MANGO PICKLE WITH DRY RED CHILLIES (*AAM AUR SOOKHI LAAL MIRCH KA ACHAAR*)

Ingredients

½ kilo hard, green, raw mangoes (wash, wipe dry, and remove the stones, and cut the mangoes into 2.5 cm pieces, approx.)
50 g (or less) red dry whole chillies (remove the stems and wipe the chillies with a dry cloth)
1 tsp hing *(roasted)*
3 tsp cumin seeds (lightly roasted)
2 tsp kalonji *seeds (onion seeds, lightly roasted)*
2 tsp turmeric powder (lightly roasted)
3 tbs salt
7–8 tbs oil (to be added to the pickle the next day.)

METHOD

Mix together all the ingredients in a glass or steel bowl.

If you do not wish to use 50 g chillies, just add 7–8 whole chillies for flavour and taste.

On the second day, add the oil, transfer the pickle to a glass jar and keep covered. (Ensure there is enough oil in the jar to cover the contents. Add a little more oil if necessary.)

Shake the jar every day, ensuring the lid is on tightly.

The pickle will be ready in 2–3 weeks time. It has a wonderful aroma and taste.

MIXED VEGETABLE PICKLE
(*MILI JULI SABAZI KA ACHAAR*)

This pickle is very tasty and is a good accompaniment with most dishes. It will stay fresh for approximately one week after it is ready.

Ingredients

1 medium cauliflower (cut the florets into small pieces lengthwise)
2 turnips (washed and cut into thin slices)
4 carrots (washed and sliced lengthwise)
8 small radishes or 1 horseradish (sliced thinly in rounds)
1 tsp hing *(roasted)*
2 tbs cumin seeds
3 tbs ground mustard seeds
1 tbs turmeric powder
1 tsp chilli powder
3 tsp salt
6–7 tbs oil

METHOD

All the vegetables should be lightly steamed and dried on a kitchen towel.

Mix all the vegetables together in a large glass bowl with the roasted *hing*, cumin seeds, ground mustard seeds, turmeric and chilli powder, salt and oil.

Leave for 4–5 days, but stir twice daily with a dry spoon. Keep covered.

The pickle will be ready to eat when it starts giving a slightly pungent, sour fragrance. It has a lovely taste and is a good accompaniment with most food. Once it is ready, it must be eaten within approximately 5–6 days.

RED CHILLI PICKLE
(*LAAL MIRCH KA ACHAAR*)

Ingredients

500 g large fresh red chillies (washed and cut into medium-sized pieces)
2 tbs mustard seeds (ground)
2 lemons (juice)
sunflower oil
2 tbs salt
½ tsp hing *(dry roasted)*

METHOD

Mix together all the ingredients (except the lemon juice) in a large glass bowl. When well mixed, place in a wide-rimmed jar and shake well. The chillies should be ¾ covered with oil, allowing space for shaking.

On the second day, add the lemon juice, mix well and shake. Leave it for 1 week, but shake it regularly.

This delicious pickle is a good accompaniment with any kind of food.

It will be hot, so use it only in small amounts – just 1 or 2 pieces at a time. Always use a clean, dry spoon for serving the pickle.

Consume within two to three weeks after it is ready.

BOILED OR ROASTED GREEN MANGO SAUCE (*AAM PANAA*)

Boiled or roasted mango sauce (*aam panaa*) is made of raw green mangoes. Its consistency is thinner than that of a sauce. It is believed to be very effective against sunstroke if taken as a drink.

Ingredients

1 green mango (large)
4–5 sprigs of mint (discard the stems, wash and chop the leaves)
3 tbs sugar
1 tsp salt
2 tsp cumin seeds (dry roasted and ground or just crushed)
2 cups water (approx.)
pinch of hing *(roasted)*

METHOD

Boil the mango or roast it on charcoal, in the oven or on a gas flame.

When it is tender, peel it, make it into a pulp with your hand and remove the stone. Discard the peel and stone.

Mash it well and mix it with the water. If it is too thick you can add more water to make it into a thin sauce.

Add the salt, sugar, red chilli, mint, roasted cumin seeds and *hing*. Serve chilled. It is very good in summer. You can serve it as an appetiser or use it as a fresh sauce with your food.

Sweet Dishes

FRESH FRUITS

GULABJAMUN AND *KULFI*

Sweet Dishes

Sweet Dishes

Sweet dishes provide energy, although you should not eat too many. They can be served on special occasions or after dinner or lunch. They can also be served as snacks at teatime, or even at breakfast time.

There are many varieties of sweet dishes. In this section, I am giving the recipes for just a few of them. Some people are allergic to nuts, which are contained in some of these recipes, so should avoid them.

ALMOND ICE CREAM
(*BADAAM KULFI*)

Ingredients

1 litre soya milk
1 cup whole almonds (soaked for 2 hours approx. in warm water and peeled)
½ cup milk
1 cup flaked almonds (available in shops)
1 cup sugar
5–6 cardamoms (discard the husk and crush the seeds)

METHOD
Liquidise the whole almonds with ½ cup of soya milk.

Boil the soya milk in a saucepan and add the liquidised almonds and mix. Let them simmer until only ¾ of the original quantity remains, add the sugar, crushed cardamom seeds and flaked almonds and mix well.

Freeze it in *kulfi* containers (cone-shaped tin containers available in Indian stores). If you do not have them, use ice trays.

When frozen, cut into pieces and serve.

BAKED BANANAS (*BHUNE KELE*)

Ingredients

3 ripe and firm bananas (peeled and cut into thick round slices)
2 tbs brown sugar
½ cup coconut or almonds (roasted and ground – optional)
1 tsp cardamom seeds (ground)
3 tbs vegan margarine (melted)
2–3 tbs soya milk

METHOD

Warm the soya milk, margarine and ground cardamom. Keep it aside. Arrange the banana slices in an ovenproof dish and spoon the mixture of milk, margarine and cardamom over the bananas. Sprinkle with sugar and bake for 15–20 minutes on gas mark 5.

Sprinkle with coconut or almonds and serve.

CARROT AND ALMOND HALWA (*GAAJAR AUR BADAAM KA HALWA*)

Ingredients

*500 g carrots (*gaajar – scraped, washed and grated)
*225 g almonds (*badaam – soaked overnight, peeled and liquidised
with approx. ½ cup of water)
10 sliced almonds (for decoration – optional)
3–4 strands of saffron (soaked in lukewarm water or soya milk)
2–3 cardamoms (remove the husk and crush the seeds)
250 g sugar
3–4 tbs vegetable ghee (or vegan margarine)
250 g soya milk

METHOD

Heat the vegetable ghee or margarine in a frying pan. Fry the crushed cardamom seeds and soaked saffron for a couple of seconds and add the grated carrots and soya milk.

When the carrots are soft and quite dry add the ground almond paste. Add a little more vegetable ghee or margarine if needed.

Fry until it is pale gold and gives a roasting aroma. Mix in the sugar and cook for another 5 minutes.

Serve as a dessert or just as a snack – hot or cold.

SEMOLINA HALWA (*SUJI KA HALWA*)

Ingredients

¾ cup semolina
½ cup vegetable ghee
¾ cup sugar
¼ cup crushed almonds (optional)
¼ cup raisins
4–5 cardamoms (discard the husk and crush the seeds)
3 cups water

METHOD

Fry the semolina in vegetable *ghee* or vegan margarine. When it gives a roasting aroma, add the raisins, crushed almonds and ground cardamom seeds.

Add the water. When it starts to boil add the sugar and cook for approximately 5 minutes until it thickens.

Transfer to a serving dish and decorate with crushed almonds.

CHILLED MELON CUBES
(*THANDA KHARBOOZA*)

Melon is a very juicy and delicious fruit. The aroma of melon is very sweet and pleasant.

Ingredients

1 honeydew melon or any variety (peeled and cut into 2.5 cm cubes)
2–3 tbs sugar
2 tbs mint leaves (washed and chopped – optional)

METHOD

Arrange the melon cubes in a large bowl, sprinkle with sugar and mix well. Chill in the fridge for 2–3 hours.

Decorate with mint leaves (if used) and serve in a fruit dish.

COCONUT FUDGE
(*NAARIYAL BURFI*)

Ingredients

2 cups desiccated coconut
1 cup sugar
1 cup soya milk
½ cup sultanas
1 tsp oil or vegan margarine

METHOD

Roast the coconut in oil, in a frying pan on medium heat for 2 minutes. Keep it aside.

Put the soya milk and sugar together in a saucepan and boil on a medium heat until it becomes ¾ of the quantity or it coats a spoon thickly. Add the sultanas and simmer for 2 minutes.

Mix the roasted coconut with the milk and sultanas and spread this mixture over the base of a greased round dish.

When it is completely cool, cut it into squares or diamond shapes.

It is delicious served as a snack or dessert.

GRAM FLOUR FUDGE
(*BESAN BURFI*)

Ingredients

*2 cups gram flour (*besan*)*
1 cup sugar (for syrup)
2–3 cardamoms (remove the husk and crush the seeds)
½ cup vegetable ghee or vegan margarine
½ cup roasted almonds or cashew nuts (crushed – optional)
1 cup soya milk

METHOD

Fry the gram flour with the vegetable *ghee* (available at Indian grocer's) or margarine. Keep stirring.

When pale gold in colour and starting to give a roasting aroma, remove from the heat and keep it aside.

Place the milk and sugar together in a saucepan. Boil on a medium heat until it becomes ¾ of the quantity or the mixture coats a spoon.

Allow the syrup to cool a little, then add it to the roasted gram flour and mix well.

Add the almonds or cashews, mix well, then spread it over the base of a pre-greased round dish and let it cool a little.

Cut into small diamond or square shapes. When it is completely cool, serve as a snack or dessert.

GULAB JAAMUN – BREADCRUMBS

Ingredients

3 large slices white bread (make soft breadcrumbs in a grinder)
½ cup soya milk (approx.)
3–4 pods cardamom (remove the husk and crush the seeds well)
¼ tsp bicarbonate of soda
1 tbs oil
2 cups sugar for syrup
2 cups water
vegetable ghee or oil for deep frying

METHOD

Syrup

Heat the water, sugar and crushed cardamom together in a saucepan.

When it starts boiling, lower the heat and simmer for 1–2 minutes (to make a thin syrup). When ready keep it aside.

Gulab jaamun

Place the breadcrumbs, bicarbonate of soda and 1 tablespoon of oil in a bowl, and add the soya milk gradually, stirring well to make a dough-like mixture.

Knead well until smooth but firm.

Break it into pieces (approximately 15–16). Make into balls with your palm (approximately 1.5 cm in diameter).

Heat the ghee or oil in a wok to medium heat. Fry 5–6 balls at a time. Keep turning until they become golden brown in colour.

Remove from the wok and put them in the syrup.

Leave for 5–6 hours. Serve warm or chilled as a snack or dessert.

GULAAB JAAMUN – SWEET POTATO (*SHAKERKANDI KE GULAB JAAMUN*)

Ingredients
Makes approximately 25

250 g sweet potatoes (boiled, peeled and mashed)
3 slices white bread (made into breadcrumbs in a grinder)
4–5 cardamoms (remove the husk and crush the seeds finely)
3 cups sugar (for syrup)
4 cups water
vegetable ghee *or oil for frying*

METHOD

Syrup

Boil the water and sugar in a saucepan for approximately 5 minutes to make a thin syrup. Keep it aside.

Gulab jaamun

Mash the boiled sweet potatoes, mix thoroughly with the white breadcrumbs and knead well.

Break the mixture into pieces and make them into balls (smaller than a golf ball) with your palm.

Heat the ghee or oil in a wok to medium heat. Fry 8–10 balls of the mixture at a time until golden brown.

Remove from the heat and put them in the syrup. Leave for 4–5 hours and then serve warm or chilled.

MANGO DELIGHT (*AAM SWAADA*)

You can buy mango pulp at an Indian grocer's or you can make it by mashing ripe mangoes.

Ingredients

250 g mango pulp
1 cup soya cream
3–4 cardamoms (remove the husks and crush the seeds)
100 g glazed cherries (halved)
2 tbs sugar

METHOD

Mix the mango pulp and soya cream together in a large bowl, add the crushed cardamom seeds and sugar, and mix well.

Decorate with the cherries, chill and serve.

SLICED MANGOES (*AAM KE KATRE*)

After dinner you can serve ripe sliced mangoes (Indian) as a sweet dish. Believe me, these are really yummy. You will soon develop a taste for them.

Ingredients

*6 ripe mangoes (*alfanso, dussheri *or any other type of Indian mango)*
1 cup soya cream

METHOD

Slice the mangoes and remove the stones. Serve the slices with or without cream. Use a spoon to eat the flesh out of the skin.

You can buy mangoes from Indian grocers, usually from May to September.

PEARS IN SYRUP
(*CHAASHNI MEIN NAASHPAATI*)

Ingredients

*6 pears, firm but not fully ripened (peel them if you wish, and cut
each into 4 pieces lengthwise)*
2 cups water
10–12 almonds (roasted and crushed – optional)
6 tbs sugar
1 stick cinnamon

METHOD

Boil the water and sugar together with the cinnamon stick
to make a thin syrup.

Add the pears to the syrup and simmer for 5–6 minutes.
Remove the pears and put them in a deep, broad dish.

Leave to cool, sprinkle with almonds and serve.

RICE KHEER (*CHAAWAL KI KHEER*)

This *kheer* is an Indian speciality. It can be served hot or chilled and it looks lovely decorated with chopped pistachios or blanched, thinly sliced almonds.

Ingredients

½ cup basmati rice (picked over, and washed 3–4 times in cold water)
1 ½ litre soya milk
3–4 cardamoms (remove the husk and crush the seeds as finely as possible)
2 tbs raisins (picked over and washed)
1 tbs sugar
3–4 flakes of saffron (soaked in 2 tbs soya milk for at least half an hour)

METHOD

Boil the soya milk in a saucepan, add the rice, then simmer. Stir and add a little water if necessary.

When the rice is quite soft add the crushed cardamom seeds, raisins and saffron (including the soya milk it was soaked in).

Add the sugar and simmer for approximately 5 minutes on medium heat. Keep stirring to prevent burning. Remove from the heat when it thickens.

Decorate with chopped almonds and pistachios and serve hot or chilled.

SEMOLINA KHEER (*SUJI KI KHEER*)

Ingredients

2 tbs coarse semolina
500 ml soya milk
1 cardamom (husk removed and seeds crushed as finely as possible)
1 tbs raisins (cleaned and washed)
2 tbs sugar
9–10 roasted cashew nuts (chopped – optional) or 9–10 almonds
(soaked, peeled and sliced – optional)

METHOD

Roast the semolina without any oil in a frying pan. Keep stirring until it gives a roasted aroma and looks pale gold in colour. Keep it aside.

Boil the soya milk in a fairly large saucepan (as milk can boil over very quickly). Turn the heat down to very low.

Mix the semolina with a little water and add to the milk. Turn the heat up and bring to the boil, then lower it again and simmer for 5–10 minutes.

Add the cardamom seeds, raisins and sugar and simmer for another 5 minutes until it becomes thick. Let it cool.

Serve in a deep dish with very finely chopped cashew nuts or almonds.

STRAWBERRIES WITH SOYA CREAM

This is a lovely dessert for summertime, cool and delicious.

Ingredients

500 g strawberries (washed, hulled and cut into halves or quarters)
3–4 tbs sugar
250 ml soya cream (optional)

METHOD

Mix together the strawberries and sugar in a bowl.
Chill in the fridge. Serve with cream.

SWEET PANCAKES (*MAALPUA*)

Ingredients

1 cup plain flour
250 ml soya milk or water (2 cups approx.)
2 tbs sugar
2 cardamoms (remove husks and crush the seeds)
golden syrup or a little sugar (for sprinkling)

METHOD

Batter

Make a batter with the flour, soya milk (add gradually), sugar and crushed cardamom seeds. The batter should have a pouring consistency.

Heat some oil on a griddle and add 1 ladle of batter. Spread into a circle approximately 13 cm in diameter.

Reduce the heat a little and smear some oil on the edges of the pancake. Turn over and cook in the same way until golden brown on both sides. Repeat with the rest of the batter.

Serve hot or cold, either with golden syrup or a little sugar. They can also be served with strawberry jam and soya cream or ice cream. If using strawberry jam, omit the cardamoms.

SWEET RICE (*MEETHE CHAAWAL*)

Ingredients

1 cup basmati rice (picked over and washed)
1½ cups sugar
½ cup sultanas or raisins
2–3 cardamoms (remove the husks and crush the seeds)
5–6 strands of saffron (soaked in water – optional)
8–10 almonds (soaked, peeled and flaked – optional)
1 tbs vegetable ghee *or vegan margarine*
2 ¼ cups water

METHOD

Heat the *ghee* or margarine in a deep saucepan and fry the crushed cardamoms.

Add the rice, sultanas or raisins, soaked saffron and water, and cover with a lid. When it starts to boil, reduce the heat.

When the rice is soft, add the sugar and mix it in carefully so that the grains of rice will not break.

Cover again and simmer for 3–4 minutes on a low heat, then stir it with a fork and check if ready to serve.

Decorate with roasted, crushed almonds.

Drinks

Drinks

Drinks

INDIAN-STYLE COFFEE

Coffee is a universal social drink. Too much coffee is not considered good for us as it contains caffeine. The Indian method of making coffee is different from the western method.

Ingredients
3 cups water
1 cup soya milk
3 tsp sugar (according to taste)
3 tsp instant coffee
2 tsp brown sugar
2 tsp cocoa powder

METHOD

Boil the water and milk together in a saucepan. When it starts boiling add the coffee and simmer for 1 minute.

Pour the coffee into cups. Add sugar according to taste.

Top it with a dash of coffee powder, brown sugar and cocoa powder.

It is delicious. Serve it after dinner.

MANGO MILKSHAKE

Ingredients

1 cup mango pulp (when in season, you can make the pulp yourself from fresh, ripened mangoes of your choice, otherwise you can buy it from any supermarket or Asian grocer's)
3 tbs sugar
5 cups soya milk
4–5 cardamom pods (remove the husk and crush the seeds)
4–5 strands saffron
ice cubes

METHOD

Mix all the ingredients together in a liquidiser or with a hand whisk.

Serve in tall glasses with ice cubes.

LEMON DRINK (*NIMBU PAANI*)

Soft drinks are very popular. Fruit juice, lemonade and cordials are all refreshing drinks, but you should not drink too many as they may harm gums and teeth.

In hot weather lemon water is very good to quench the thirst, and also has a cooling effect. It can be made spicy or sweet and sour.

SPICY LEMON DRINK (*MASAALA NIMBU PAANI*)

Ingredients

4 glasses water in a jug
3 lemons (juice)
½ tsp salt
1 tsp black pepper (freshly ground)
1 tsp cumin seeds (roasted and ground)
ice cubes

METHOD

Mix all the ingredients with the water in the jug.

Serve with the ice cubes. This is a very appetising drink.

SWEET AND SOUR LEMON DRINK (*KHATTA MEETHA NIMBU PAANI*)

Ingredients

4 glasses water in a jug
4 tbs sugar (according to taste – you could add more sugar or 2 tbs syrup)
3 lemons (juice)
ice cubes (optional)

METHOD

Mix together the water, sugar (or syrup) and lemon juice thoroughly. Serve in tall tumblers with ice cubes. This is a very refreshing drink.

TEA

Tea was discovered in China a very long time ago. It is a versatile drink and popular all over the world. As it contains caffeine it is a mild stimulant. It is considered to be good for alertness and digestion.

There are many ways of taking tea, for example, black tea, tea with soya milk and tea with lemon. In India, tea is quite popular with cardamom seeds, fennel seeds or ginger. These types of tea are said to be healthy and good for digestion.

It is better not to take tea with meals because it reduces the absorption of vitamins.

TEA WITH CARDAMOM
(*ILLAICHEE CHAI*)

Make ordinary tea and infuse with 2 cardamom pods (remove the husks, take out the seeds, crush them and add to the brewing tea). It is tasty and full of aroma.

TEA WITH FENNEL SEEDS
(*SAUNF CHAI*)

Make ordinary tea and add 7–8 fennel seeds (crushed). This tea is said to be good for digestion and a remedy for colds.

TEA WITH GINGER (ADRAK CHAI)

Ingredients

4 cups water (for 4 cups)
1 cm ginger (peeled, washed and chopped)
2 tea bags or 3 tsp loose tea
sugar (optional)
soya milk (optional)

METHOD

If you are boiling the water in a saucepan, add the ginger as well.

If you are boiling the water in a kettle, brew the tea in a teapot with the pieces of ginger. Serve as usual.

This tea is very good for the digestion and is believed to be a good remedy for colds or pains.

TEA WITH LEMON (*NIMBU CHAI*)

Make tea in the usual way, but instead of adding soya milk, add a few drops of fresh lemon juice.

This is very good for slimmers. The lemon flavour gives freshness in the morning. It is a good remedy for colds because it contains vitamin C.

Menus

Menus

It is very important in a vegan diet to include pulses (lentils, dried peas and beans), vegetables, rice or bread, and salad every day. The following menus are just a few examples. You can alter them according to your taste. In the menus, *daal* means any cooked pulse or bean dish.

LUNCHES

- *Aaloo paraathas* and tomato chutney
- *Cheelas*, mango or lemon pickle and salad
- *Pooris* and fried chickpeas
- Vegetable *pakoras*, horseradish salad, herb chutney and sliced bread
- Vegetable *samosas*, vegetable salad and sweet mango chutney

EVENING MEALS

It is not necessary to have both bread and rice with every evening meal. You could have just bread or just rice, or bread and rice if you wish.

Menu one

- Salad – mixed *kachoomar*
- Vegetable – *aaloo gobhi*
- Daal – moong *daal* with mint and coriander chutney
- Rice – plain rice
- Bread – *chapaatis* or *paraathas*
- Dessert – fruit salad or bananas and roasted coconut and almonds

Menu two

- Salad – vegetable and sunflower seed salad
- Vegetable – spicy roasted aubergine
- Daal – *masoor daal* with mango pickle
- Rice – plain rice
- Bread – *chapaatis*
- Dessert – semolina *kheer*

Menu three

- Salad – beetroot salad
- Vegetable – masaala potatoes and peas
- Daal – dry *urad daal* with mango pickle or chutney
- Rice – plain rice
- Bread – *chapaatis, paraathas* or *pooris*
- Dessert – sliced mangoes

Menu four

- Salad – mixed vegetable salad
- Vegetable – French beans and potatoes
- Daal – masaala chickpeas and potatoes
- Rice – onion pilau
- Bread – *chapaatis* or *naan*
- Dessert – strawberries with or without soya cream

Menu five

- Salad – mixed vegetable salad
- Vegetable – spicy yam
- Daal – masaala *chana daal* with tomatoes
- Rice – plain rice
- Bread – *chapaatis* or *paraathas*
- Dessert – chilled melon cubes

TASTY PARTY MENUS FOR SPECIAL OCCASIONS

Menu one

- Starter – *aaloo chaat*, cocktail samosas
- Salad – carrot and radish salad
- Vegetable – masaala okra (*bhindi*)
- Daal – moong *daal* and spinach
- Rice – onion pilau
- Bread – *chapaatis*
- Dessert – carrot and almond *halwa*

Menu two

- Starter – vegetable *pakoras*
- Salad – vegetable and sunflower seed salad
- Vegetable – *aaloo gobhi*, deep fried aubergine
- Daal – chick peas with vegetables
- Rice – pea (*matar*) pilau
- Bread – plain *pooris* or *chapaatis*
- Dessert – almond *kulfi*

Menu three

- Starter – *aaloo tikki*, Bombay mix
- Salad – mixed vegetable salad
- Vegetable – masaala *baingan*, cabbage and peas
- Daal – *masoor daal* with mango pickle
- Rice – plain rice
- Bread – *paraathas* or *chapaatis*
- Dessert – rice *kheer* and fresh sliced mangoes

Menu four

- Starter – vegetable *pakoras*
- Salad – pasta salad
- Vegetable – masaala potatoes and masaala aubergine
- Daal – kidney beans
- Rice – mushroom pilau
- Bread – *chapaatis*
- Dessert – *gulab jaamun* and strawberries with soya cream

Menu five

- Starter – bread cutlets and Bombay mix
- Salad – mushroom and broccoli and mixed *kachoomar*
- Vegetable – stuffed peppers, and potatoes and peas with onion masaala
- Daal – moong *daal*
- Rice – potato pilau
- Bread – *chapaatis* or *naan*
- Dessert – semolina *halwa* and sliced mango

Index

Index

Printed in the United Kingdom
by Lightning Source UK Ltd.
122441UK00001B/36/A